OUR ARMY AT WAR

OUR ARMY AT WAR

THE STORY OF AMERICAN CAMPAIGNS IN WORLD WAR II TOLD IN OFFICIAL WAR DEPARTMENT PHOTOGRAPHS

WITH AN INTRODUCTION BY

GENERAL GEORGE C. MARSHALL

CHIEF OF STAFF OF THE UNITED STATES ARMY

HARPER & BROTHERS · PUBLISHERS

NEW YORK   LONDON

℃ Unless otherwise noted, all photographs in this book have been made by official U. S. Army photographers of the Signal Corps, the Air Forces, and the War Department Bureau of Public Relations. The maps are provided by the Army publication, Newsmap.

OUR ARMY AT WAR

7-4

CONTENTS

●

Introduction by General George C. Marshall

I. The Campaign in the Pacific and Far East *Legends* 1-174

II. The Campaign in the Aleutians   "   175-240

III. The Mediterranean Campaign

    The Campaign in North Africa   "   241-314

    The Campaign in Sicily   "   315-366

    The Campaign in Italy   "   367-417

IV. The Campaign in the Air Over Europe   "   418-482

●

INTRODUCTION

THIS book is a photographic record of the United States Army's first two years at war—a period that has witnessed the growth of our military forces from a small Army to more than seven-and-a-half million men and women. The battle scenes and glimpses of the life of the combat soldier have been arranged with a view to presenting a graphic picture of the conditions under which American soldiers are living and the sacrifices they are making in this worldwide struggle.

These pictures should serve as an inspiration to Americans. They are evidence of the willingness and the ability of a democratic people to arm themselves and fight for the great principle of democracy. They are positive evidence of the obligation of the American people to support their armed forces without stint or selfish quibble.

I

THE CAMPAIGN IN THE PACIFIC
AND THE FAR EAST

JAPAN drew first blood in the sneak attack on Pearl Harbor and pressed the advantage of surprise to invade our outposts in the Far East. Available United States forces were quickly called to the first task at hand—the reinforcement of garrisons along our West Coast and in Panama, Hawaii, and Alaska. Within ten days critical areas on both coasts of the United States had been provided with a reasonable degree of protection against air and sea attack. Within five weeks, more than 600,000 troops with their guns and equipment were moved according to plan to ports of embarkation and to tactical posts.

Immediately after Pearl Harbor, when Germany and Italy also declared war on the United States, we found ourselves plunged into a global conflict in which our lines of communication encircled the earth, extending over 56,000 miles. In the first critical period it was necessary for us to establish without delay large supply bases in Australia for both air and ground troops to counter the first great surge of the Japanese offensive. By June, 1942, 150,000 Army troops, as well as Marines and Navy ground echelons, had been established in the South and Southwest Pacific Areas.

Meanwhile, at home, military leaders set themselves to the tremendous task of building and training an armed force of more than seven million. The expansion was such as to stagger the imagination. Our officer corps grew from 93,000 to 521,000; service units of the Army Air Forces expanded by 12,000 per cent; the Engineers by 4,000 per cent. Simplification of command and decentralization of authority were accomplished early in 1942 when the President and Secretary of War approved a reorganization which established three great commands under the direct supervision of the Chief of Staff—the Army Air Forces, Army Ground Forces, and Army Service Forces.

As the Japanese overran the Philippines, the Netherlands East Indies, the Malay Peninsula, and Burma, America's giant industrial plant, now geared to war production, rapidly gained momentum.

For both Great Britain and the United States, military operations in the Pacific Area and Far East created unprecedented shipping problems. To land and maintain American forces in Australia required more than twice the ship tonnage necessary for similar American forces in Europe or North Africa. Immediate, effective defense was vital to Australia, with 4,500 miles of frontier exposed to possible Japanese landings. And the Japs were within striking distance.

In February 1942, General Douglas MacArthur was instructed by the War Department to proceed to Australia to assume command of the newly-designated Southwest Pacific Area. His directive from the Combined Chiefs of Staff included the missions of holding Australia, checking the enemy's advance along the Melanesian Barrier, protecting land, sea, and air communications with the Southwest Pacific, and maintaining our position in the Philippines. The last was not to be accomplished, though the gallant defense by our forces under Lieut. Gen. Jonathan M. Wainwright is an epic of our history. Bataan and Corregidor are scheduled stops on the road back.

Our growing air power in the Southwest

Pacific turned the tide of battle against the Japanese and put them first on the defensive, then into retreat. Long-range bombing missions were successful against the enemy in the Solomons and New Guinea. These were followed up by the ground forces which proceeded to drive the Japs back northward.

General Marshall thus summarizes the campaign: "In the South and Southwest Pacific two facts are plainly evident to the Japanese command as well as to the world at large: Our progress may seem slow, but it is steady and determined, and it has been accompanied by a terrific destruction of enemy planes and surface vessels. This attrition must present an appalling problem for the enemy high command."

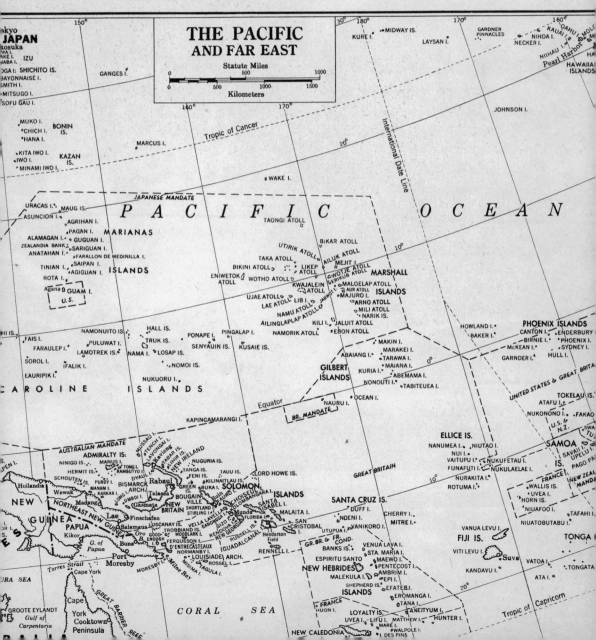

THE PACIFIC
AND FAR EAST

Statute Miles

Kilometers

1. On Dec. 7, 1941 the Japanese emissaries were in Washington, talking peace. The time was ripe for Pearl Harbor!

This Navy photograph, one of the most remarkable combat pictures of all time, was made at the exact moment the U. S. Destroyer Shaw blew up in Pearl Harbor.

2. While part of the enemy air force was reducing Pearl Harbor and its magnificent warships to an inferno of fire, smoke, and twisted steel . . .

U. S. Navy photograph showing three stricken U. S. battleships. Left to right: West Virginia, severely damaged; Tennessee, damaged; and Arizona, sunk. The Japs hit 8 battleships, damaging 5 badly. Total toll in vessels: 18.

3. . . . other planes were attacking Hickam Field.

Firemen are attempting to extinguish oil flames at Hickam Field, the Army's big airbase, just outside of Honolulu. Harbor and drydock installations were converted into piles of twisted, blazing ruins.

4. Planes were blasted in their hangars or smashed on the runways before they could even take to the air to meet the treacherous Jap.

A smashed B-17-C, near Hangar No. 5, Hickam Field. Aviation hangars were blasted and gutted by bomb fragments and fire.

5. When the enemy bombers had passed, there was little left to salvage on the great airfield.

Rear view of Hangar No. 11, Hickam Field. 177 planes were destroyed. Our total dead at Pearl Harbor was 2,343, with 960 missing.

6. Simultaneously, the Japs struck without warning at . . .

Warehouse destroyed by fire from Japanese bombers at Nichols Field, Philippine Islands.

7. . . . the Philippines . . .

Cavite Navy Yard, Philippine Islands. Barge No. 181, right center, is loaded with burning torpedoes. Small arms shells are exploding in the center of the heavy blaze on the left.

8. . . . as well as at Malaya, Hong Kong, Guam, Wake, and Midway.

Casualties, most of them mechanics, after the Japs bombed the port area at Manila.

9. The Mikado's little men, prepared by years of planning, training, and producing for war, seemed to be having everything their way.

This hazy photo, from a Japanese source, shows types of their troops and equipment.

10. The United States rallied from the first blows in a great surge of wrath—but was impotent in its unpreparedness. The pathetically small garrison of Americans and Filipinos began one of the great delaying actions of history.

U. S. soldiers preparing to mine and destroy a bridge at Nasugbu, Batangas, Dec. 12, 1941.

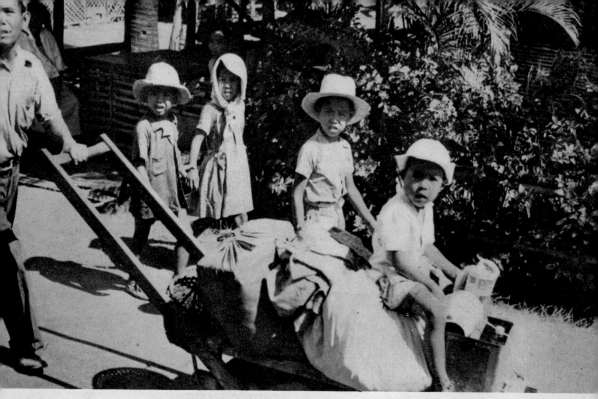

11. **The Filipinos took to the road . . .**
Evacuees leave Cavite after the first Japanese raid.

12. **. . . joining the long list of refugee peoples.**
More evacuees from Cavite.

13. Guam fell to the Jap. Then came the thrilling but tragic news of Wake Island. Manila was declared an open city. But that was merely a phrase to . . .

Looking toward Parian Gate, from Galle Anda, in the Walled City of Manila. This row of burned buildings had housed the **Philippines Herald.**

14. ... Jap fliers.

These three Japanese aviators were shot down and taken prisoner during a raid on Manila.

15. The cruel little troops of the Japanese Emperor swarmed through Borneo, the Celebes, Burma, the Malay Peninsula, the Netherlands East Indies, and New Britain Island, just north of New Guinea, which was the island shield of Australia!

Photograph from a Japanese source.

16. But the schedule was falling behind in the Philippines—in a place with the unfamiliar name of ...

These Japanese soldiers were killed by American soldiers and Philippine scouts while they were attempting to escape by climbing down the cliff at Longoskawayan Point on Bataan. The naked condition of the bodies indicates that the Japs were attempting to swim away.

17. ... Bataan. Here our men dug and held trenches that for many were destined to be their graves.

Capt. S. W. Little, Sgt. John G. Graham, Lt. P. W. Frutiger, and Cpl. R. L. Carter ducking shrapnel at Lamao, Bataan, while the ammunition dump blazes after a bombing by the Japs.

18. While Uncle Sam grimly prepared for the day of final reckoning with the Japs, Americans and Filipinos, bought time for him and paid for it with their blood.

Filipino fighters await medical attention on Bataan.

19. Our soldiers knew that the barrier they erected was doomed to failure—but for them there was only one thing to do: FIGHT!

Tank traps set up by American troops on Bataan.

20. While armchair strategists at home screamed for reinforcements for Bataan, our transports began to slip out of West Coast ports for the South Pacific.

These U. S. Army men of a headquarters company are getting into barges in a harbor at New Caledonia, following their voyage from Australia.

21. But the way to Bataan was blocked. Its defenders continued to take one of the historic poundings of all time.

Destruction on Bataan Peninsula caused by Japanese bombs and shells.

TICKET TO ARMISTICE

USE THIS TICKET, SAVE YOUR LIFE
YOU WILL BE KINDLY TREATED

Follow These Instructions:

1. Come towards our lines waving a white flag.
2. Strap your gun over your left shoulder muzzle down and pointed behind you.
3. Show this ticket to the sentry.
4. Any number of you may surrender with this one ticket.

JAPANESE ARMY HEADQUARTERS

投　降、票

此ノ票ヲ持ツモノハ投降者ナリ
投降者ヲ殺害スルヲ嚴禁ス

大 日 本 軍 司 令 官

Sing your way to Peace pray for Peace

22, 23. The Japs, imitating western technique—and doing it badly—dropped crude propaganda leaflets behind the defenders' lines.

The one below illustrates the Japs' mistaken notion that a siren's song would induce the Filipinos to lay down their arms.

Don't wait to die

Before the bombs fall, let me take your hand and kiss your gentle cheeks and murmur ...

Before the terror comes, let me walk beside you in garden deep in petalled sleep ...

Let me, while there is still a time and place. Feel soft against me and rest ... rest your warm hand on my breast ...

Come home to me, and dream with me...

24. While our troops fought to the point of exhaustion, the Japs tried the Axis line of "Divide and Conquer" . . .

Cpl. Ray "Slats" Spencer, motorcycle dispatch rider, catches a cat nap on Bataan, his weapons carefully arranged for instant use if needed.

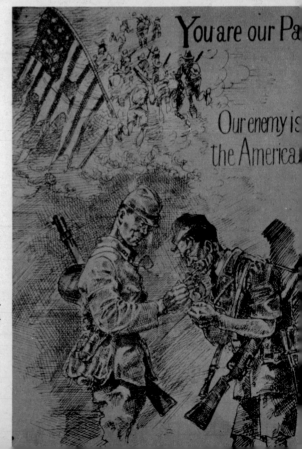

25. . . . with these leaflets dropped from the air for Filipino soldiers.

26. Friends? The Filipino thought of his women-
folk and remembered the sack and horrors of
Nanking. He answered the leaflets with...

A family of refugees finds shelter on Bataan in a lean-to
made of bamboo and grass.

27. ... bullets.

Dead Japanese soldiers at Longoskawayan Point,
Bataan.

28. But the Jap had lives to spare, and plenty of paper. He dropped more leaflets, offering safety and dishonor to a stock which had bred heroes.

Capt. Art Wermuth, the "one-man army" of Bataan, shown here with his Filipino aide, is credited with the annihilation of many Japs.

29. The glorious defense of Bataan continued through four long months of bitter, sweating, gory jungle warfare.

(Back home, America was rushing full speed ahead to change peace-loving citizens into soldiers. These are infantry trainees at Camp Roberts, Calif., a huge Replacement Training Center, getting calisthenics as part of their basic training.)

30. During that time, the Japs took Singapore, cut the Burma Road to China, and, with the Battle of the Java Sea, began their invasion of Java.

(In America, at Camp San Luis Obispo, Calif., these soldiers were the nucleus of the 1st Filipino Battalion trained in the U. S.)

31. They took Bali, Timor, Sumatra, the Andamans, Lae and Salamaua on New Guinea, and were now in the Solomons—spearhead to Australia.

(In America, men were learning to handle machine guns. This 30-mm Browning gun is manned by Pvt. I. J. Schaffler and assistant gunner Pvt. J. Werchicofsky, both of New York, and both of the 34th Infantry, 8th Division, Ft. Jackson.)

32. The Southwest Pacific had become one great disaster for the United Nations.

(In America, men of the North and the South learned to charge together over hills and country-sides made famous by Stonewall Jackson and other Civil War generals.)

33. For the dwindling, unsupplied force at Bataan, battered by a constantly increasing horde of invaders ...

(In America, men learned the intricacies of the mortar.)

34. ... there could be only one end:

(In America, men were getting tougher day by day and a powerful new army was coming rapidly into being.)

35. **The surrender of Bataan came on April 9, 1942.**

(In America, men learned to search the skies for enemy planes. Cpl. Robert Anderson of Pennington, Va., is No. 1 sight and elevation man and Pvt. Clarence Flunk, of Lansdale, Pa., is No. 2 sight man.)

36. Bataan was the severest defeat ever suffered by the United States in overseas combat.

(In America, troops in training at Fort George G. Meade, Md., sang as they returned from an early morning march.)

37. 30,000 American and Filipino troops were taken prisoner ...

(In America, this crew was learning to load a 155mm. gun, their rookie days fast fading into the past.)

38. 3,000 got away to Corregidor—the last foothold of resistance in the Philippines.

(In America, the new army was getting to know its business in a big way. This unit is completely motorized, consisting of three 37mm. batteries, a 75mm. battery, one Infantry battalion, one Engineer platoon, one Anti-Tank platoon, all equipped with radio communication.)

39. Nine days after the fall of Bataan, on Apr. 18, 1942, Jimmy Doolittle's men roared in from the sea to bomb Tokyo.

This photo of Yokosuka Naval Base was taken from a B-25. Note the Japanese naval vessels in the foreground.

40. The road to that citadel of aggression was still long and hard, but these American bombers reminded Tojo that there *was* such a road, and that American feet would one day be on it.

The crew of Gen. James Doolittle's own bombing plane, pictured with Chinese friends after the U. S. airmen bailed out over China. Left to right: Staff Sgt. F. A. Braemer, bombardier, Seattle; Staff Sgt. P. J. Leonard, engineer-gunner, Denver; Lt. R. E. Cole, co-pilot, Dayton; Gen. Doolittle, pilot; and Lt. H. A. Potter, navigator, Pierre, S. D. (Sgt. Leonard has since been killed in action in North Africa.) These men were more fortunate than some of their comrades, who came down in Japanese-held territory and were executed in complete violation of the international rules of war observed by civilized nations.

41. While Bataan had been taking it, American military strategists had been doing first things first, reinforcing our garrisons on the West Coast and in Panama, Hawaii, and Alaska. Now, while Americans huddled in the bomb shelters of Corregidor, other Americans swarmed onto the shores of New Caledonia—on the flank of our vital supply route to Australia.

Natives of New Caledonia dance for American troops. They are fond of the soldiers and have relaxed many a tribal taboo for their entertainment. Note the soldier in center of circle.

42. On the day little girls back home were dancing around their Maypoles, Lt. Gen. Joseph W. Stilwell led his men on the long hike out of Burma to escape the advancing Japs.

Gen. Stilwell ended his famous march twenty days later in Imphal, Assam. Behind Gen. Stilwell in this photo are his two aides, Lt. Col. Frank Dorn and Lt. Richard Young.

43. Cut off from news of the world, Gen. Stilwell and his men could not know, on the fifth day of their hike, that Corregidor, last foothold in the Philippines, had just fallen, or that America was winning a great naval battle in the Coral Sea, beating back a Jap thrust at Australia on the Pacific supply line to the Antipodes.

Nobody in the Stilwell group knew where the Japs were, and wild rumors were circulated that the enemy was coming up the Chindwin River in gunboats. Hence the first great goal of the group was the Chindwin. This picture shows the party walking across the sand approach to the river. Their rafts had been abandoned several miles back on the Uyu.

44. In its discouragements and adversities, the summer of 1942 in the Southwest Pacific can only be compared to . . .

(But, in spite of everything, the training of our new army went doggedly forward. In North Carolina, these four men in a jeep pull a 37 mm. gun over rough terrain.)

45. . . . the winter of 1779 at Valley Forge.

(In South Carolina, a machine gun crew fires on "enemy" planes as they drop their bombs.)

46. June and July paraded grimly by.

(All over America the gathering might of the nation is
beginning to show in masses of marching men.)

47. But despite a few bright spots—such as the great three-day Battle of Midway in which we smashed with heavy loss the Jap attempt to take Midway, and perhaps Hawaii—Jap expansion continued relentlessly.

(In Kentucky, part of an infantry regiment passes by on review at Camp
Breckinridge.)

48. By the end of that disastrous summer, the Japanese held the rich tip of southeastern Asia, as well as the Indies, most valuable of all colonial domains . . .

(But men of Japanese blood are not all
united behind Tojo. In America, Pvt. Take-
shi Omuro and Pfc. Kentoku Nakasone are
in training with the new army of democracy.)

49. . . . and they were at the gates of Australia and India.

Photo from a Japanese source shows their
troops and equipment in the summer of
1942.

50. The Axis, with a tremendous head start in building its war machine, with shorter lines of supply, and with 250,000,000 people dominating another 350,000,000, was at the zenith of its power.

(In America, troops were embarking for unknown destinations.)

51. Said the *New York Times* . . .

(Member of a Military Police Company boarding a transport.)

52. "Men wondered if another push by the Mikado's legions, another drive by the Fuehrer's panzers, might not break the ramparts of Central Asia. . . ."

(And these U. S. Army men were en route to Australia.)

53. ". . . If that happened," the *Times* continued, "the Allies would be cut into fragments, their three years of falling back might turn into catastrophe, and over their rout might fall the twilight of democracy and international order."

(Army and Navy heads inspect the crew of a transport which is to carry infantry troops to the Solomon Islands to reinforce the Marines. The troops aboard the ship were formerly stationed on New Caledonia. Front to rear: Vice Adm. Robert Lee Ghormley, Commanding the South Pacific area; Division Commander of the Navy [unidentified]; Capt. Charles Paul McFeaters, Ship Commander [behind Ghormley]; Maj. Gen. M. F. Harmon, Commanding the Army Forces in South Pacific area [with garrison cap]; Rear Adm. Kelly Turner; Maj. Gen. Alexander Patch, Jr., Commanding the United Forces in New Caledonia [with garrison cap].)

54. On Aug. 7, men stopped wondering long enough to note that U. S. Marines, in a surprise stroke, had landed in the Southern Solomons and had seized Tulagi and a vital new airfield on GUADALCANAL. That was the magic new word that meant the turning of the tide in the Southwest Pacific—the word that marked the beginning of Allied offensive strategy in that area.

U. S. troops go over the side of a transport to landing boats below. Mud, dense jungles, Jap troops and bombers were some of the obstacles faced by these forces after they landed.

55. At the end of August, Australians were wiping out a Jap landing force at Milne Bay on the eastern tip of New Guinea. The end of August marked the end of Jap expansion in the Southwest Pacific area—expansion which had carried the enemy within 30 miles of Port Moresby. MacArthur had begun the long fight back to Bataan! ...

Veterans of a famous Australian division open ranks for an inspection by General Douglas MacArthur, Allied Commander-in-Chief in the Southwest Pacific, at their camp "somewhere in Australia."

56. ... Back with the stalwart soldiers of an Allied Army: American, Australian, New Zealand, and Dutch.

A group of American and New Zealand soldiers exchange views and explanations of their respective weapons and tactics in New Caledonia.

57. In Australia and other bases, MacArthur piled up his equipment . . .

A U.S. Army Division leaves the parade ground in New Caledonia after being reviewed by the commanding officer, Lt. Col. Alexander George.

58. . . . and his ammunition.

Pvt. Floyd West, Pfc. Charles R. Cooper, and Pvt. Alex Williams painting hand grenades in Australia.

59. American troops were now arriving in increasi numbers to push the enemy back from his island o posts.

Members of a forward echelon loading onto a barge from th troopship, off the coast of New Guinea.

60. They were young men, grim, tough, but smiling, even in the face of jungle hardships.

The barge pulls away from the troopship and heads for the shore.

61. Their equipment was the finest of any army in the world, especially designed for combat in the jungles of the South Pacific islands.

The troops disembark, somewhere in New Guinea.

62. And with them came the inevitable supplies, in the newfangled barges of World War II —or any other conveyance that was handy. Providing transportation to the Japanese-held islands was a vast problem.

Here native canoes are pressed into service.

63. The Army came in to relieve the Marines at strategic Guadalcanal—strategic because the airfield, hacked out of its coconut groves by the Japanese before we took it, could command the supply line from the United States to Australia.

An Army jeep driving from a lighter onto Red Beach, Guadalcanal, during the landing of the Americal Division, which previously had been stationed at New Caledonia.

64. Often a military landing means blood and tears —but even when unopposed it *always* means sweat, lugging . . .

Our newly arrived troops unload rations from landing boats at Guadalcanal.

65. . . . and lugging . . .

Troops carrying sacks of flour from barges to Red Beach, Guadalcanal.

66. ... while the transports ride at anchor and a Flying Fortress overhead keeps an eye out for the enemy.

Guadalcanal.

67. Americans got to see a lot of palm trees . . .

Men of the Americal Division after debarking at Guadalcanal.

68. . . . and learned how it felt to stand under them and watch the ships they came in steam slowly away.

The Americal Division set an Army record in the Pacific Area by unloading 36,000 tons of supplies in 90 hours at Guadalcanal.

69. Then they had to turn their backs on the beach, and hack their way inland . . .

This is a typical scene in the Guadalcanal jungle.

70. . . . building roads as they went . . . .

This road is being built along a ridge close to the front lines on Guadalcanal. All equipment from this point to the front is carried by native bearers like this water carrier in the foreground.

71. ... and bridges ...

Army engineers rush to complete a heavy-traffic bridge across a Guadalcanal river in three days. Planking is laid over a framework of palm logs.

72. ... and bivouac and supply areas, and clearings for airfields.

A bivouac area and supply dump the day after the Japanese retreated before U. S. forces on Guadalcanal. Shell and bomb craters are used as fox holes by the troops.

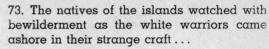

73. The natives of the islands watched with bewilderment as the white warriors came ashore in their strange craft ...

A native in his outrigger canoe gazes with astonishment at an LCT (Landing Craft Tank) during our occupation of an island in the Trobriand Group.

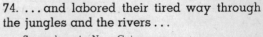

74. ... and labored their tired way through the jungles and the rivers ...

Somewhere in New Guinea.

75. . . . and the hills.

Native carriers bringing supplies up through the Guadalcanal jungles to the hills. Supplies first had to be brought by boat up a shallow river.

76. But the native was more than bewildered, he was coöperative. He pitched in on the long treks, lending his broad back . . .

Crossing a river in New Guinea.

77. ... and his knowledge of his native island.

A native of New Guinea draws a map on the ground to show the position of enemy forces. Left to right: Cpl. William Mason, Col. Kelsie Miller, Capt. John Roworth, Capt. Emil Khail.

78. The Americans had all sorts of gadgets to make noise. Some made small, sweet noises ...

Natives of Guadalcanal, who aided U. S. forces in wresting the island from Jap control, relax after the completion of the campaign and enjoy a USO record.

79. ...others made very loud noises and had the might of many warriors.

A group of Guadalcanal natives who had assisted coast watchers witnesses the firing of an anti-aircraft gun. The pit in right foreground shelters an anti-aircraft machine gun, used to protect the crew of the heavy gun from low-flying enemy planes.

80. An anthropologist would have been delighted with the interest which each race ...

Capt. Emil Khail, Two Rivers, Wis., bargains with natives for fruits and vegetables, in New Guinea.

81. ... took in the other.

A contingent of American troops landed at the Fiji Islands, British colony in the Southwest Pacific. Instead of the cannibals they had read about in their school books, they met a friendly group of natives allied in the cause of democracy. Pfc. Benjamin H. Burton, with good reason, admires the abundance of hair on this Fiji Islander's head. Some natives bleach their hair with lime and go in for elaborate headdresses.

82. It was a strange war.

Corp. Joe Harkings of Hazel Park, Mich., watches a New Guinea native demonstrate the art of drinking from a coconut.

. . . But Johnny Doughboy
[di]dn't come all this way
[on] a mission for the Na-
[tion]al Geographic Society.
[He dres]sed when necessary
[to c]amouflage . . .

A regulation Army jungle
suit, complete with equipment
and rations, worn by a soldier in New Caledonia.

84. ... Johnny was toughening up for his primary mission of ...

Somewhere in New Guinea, these men of an advanced patrol seem unconcerned about enemy gunfire directed at their position.

85. ... killing Japs.

A water-filled shell hole in New Guinea.

86. No story ever told was stranger than this true adventure of boys from Kane, Kans., Nashville, Tenn. . . .

Troops crossing a footbridge in a South Seas jungle.

87. . . . Gardner, Mass., and Walla Walla, Wash., who . . .

A Japanese breastwork taken over by Americans in New Guinea.

88. ...halted the fanatical hordes of the Japanese feudal system on soil that was alien to both armies.

Another shell hole in New Guinea.

89. It is a story of Americans pushing on boldly or warily...

This photo, made from an abandoned Japanese pillbox, shows our men advancing under fire in New Guinea.

90. ...over more dead Japs.

Japanese infantryman killed during the battle for a village in New Guinea. Our Army took the village.

91. It is a story of learning to distinguish an enemy pillbox from an innocent-looking pile of coconuts.

This was, in reality, a camouflaged Jap pillbox, captured by U. S. soldiers. The American pictured here, his gun ready for instant action, is searching the area for enemy stragglers.

92. It is a story of taking your life in your hands as you steal up on the enemy's hole in the ground ...

Soldiers firing their rifles into a Japanese dugout in New Guinea before entering it for inspection.

93. ... and of killing him before he kills you.

Dead Jap trapped in his hole. The top of the dugout is supported by logs and dirt.

94. It is a story of seeking the enemy on the beaches...

Four U. S. riflemen of a volunteer advance patrol, assigned to "feel out the enemy," are creeping up the beach with their objective just before them. These men received the DSC for this action.

95. ...and finding him...

On the coast of New Guinea.

96. . . . and exterminating him.

More Japanese dead in New Guinea.

97. If a fellow wants to live when he's up against a tough enemy, he gets pretty tough himself.

After wiping out a pocket of Japs, U. S. soldiers display some of the captured personal effects of the Japanese. Note what is tatooed on the chest of the man in the center.

98. But sometimes a dead Jap...

This one was killed when he sneaked back into a Japanese position which the Americans had taken three days before. Fanatical Japs often do this just to get one effective shot at an American, even though they know they will probably be killed themselves.

99. ...may start a soldier thinking...

Pvt. Bill Winter of Redden, Okla., cleaning reclaimed ammunition in New Guinea.

100. ...about the horror of the killing ...

Pvt. Richard Ryski of Chicago poke[?] around in the litter of equipment an[?] bones in an abandoned Jap camp o[?] Guadalcanal.

101. ...and of being killed[?]

A victim of concussion, this [?] can soldier lies dead in the [?] after a Jap air raid on Rendo[?]

102. It all goes against his American creed of live and let live.

Dead Jap in his dugout in New Guinea. Heavy jungle growth surrounding the dugout made detection difficult until shell fire denuded the area.

103. Then he remembers that this isn't something the free men of the world asked for but a fight for their own survival—as the enemy made unmistakably plain at Pearl Harbor.

While shells from Japanese artillery soar overhead, American troops heat their C rations for a meal near the front where Americans and Australians were attacking Jap positions around Salamaua, New Guinea. Left to right: Pvt. Glen F. Fuller, Leion, Ia.; Pvt. Emil Entzminger, Kulm, N. D.; Hal O'Flaherty, Chicago war correspondent; and Pvt. Harry Jones, Baltimore.

104. So when the jungle night is over . . .

Guadalcanal

105. . . . he awakes next morning and is off again on the job of killing Japs—a job which he must finish before he can go home.

Troops moving into a forward combat zone in New Guinea.

106. And, with the curiosity which has made inventor to the world, he goes about poking nose into the mechanics of it all . . .

This American soldier is having a look-see at the int of a shattered Jap vehicular water tank.

107. . . . the enemy's planes . . .

A Zero downed on Guadalcanal during the final day of enemy resistance.

108. ... his trucks ...

This one, smashed and captured by U. S. forces, was later repaired and used to transport our own supplies.

109. ... and his tanks.

These were destroyed by American shellfire on the beach at Guadalcanal.

110. Living in a jungle is dirty business ...

Pvt. Lloyd Culuck eats his B rations, using the top of the can as spoon and fork combined. When this photo was made he had not had a chance to bathe or shave in twelve days.

111. ... with none of the comforts of home.

Men bathing and washing clothes in a creek in New Guinea.

112. And after you've hiked all day ...

Men taking a breather somewhere on the trail in New Guinea.

113. ... and sweated out the chow-line, standing ankle-deep in mud ...

Men of the task force that took Rendova.

114. . . . you certainly appreciate a swim if there's one to be had.

A river on Guadalcanal.

115. It wouldn't be so bad if jungle fighting were merely inconvenience . . .

Soldiers using their steel helmets as pots to heat their food on Guadalcanal. Left to right: Pfc. Joseph Hebert, Lake Charles, La.; Pfc. Peter Rendels, Gary, Ind.

116. ... and keeping your eyes open ...

Aircraft observers watching for enemy planes from a hilltop overlooking their camp on Rendova. The Japs lost heavily here.

117. . . . and having a fast trigger finger. Those are the petty things.

A patrol crossing a jungle stream under protection of a guard.

118. We are also paying in blood . . .

Through the New Guinea jungle a wounded soldier is carried on a litter from the fighting front to a field hospital for treatment.

119. ...good American blood...

Wounded when the Japanese raided one of our airfields in New Guinea, Cpl. Henry Chum of Washington, D. C., receives plasma at a field hospital.

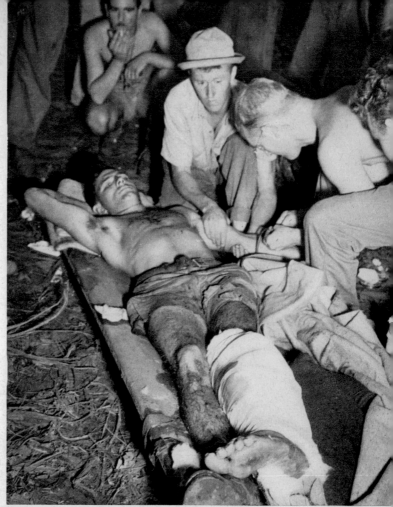

120. ...and American lives.

A dead American soldier is taken from under the wreckage of his truck on Rendova Island. He had vainly sought refuge under it when Jap bombers came over.

Wounded by a hand grenade, Pvt. Anthony Sorice is being taped up by his brother-in-law, Joseph Alderuccio. Both are from New Britain, Conn., and are members of the same infantry unit on New Georgia Island. Alderuccio and five others carried Sorice a mile through the jungle before reaching a trail built by the engineers. Here they put him on a jeep pressed into service as an ambulance, and he was later evacuated.

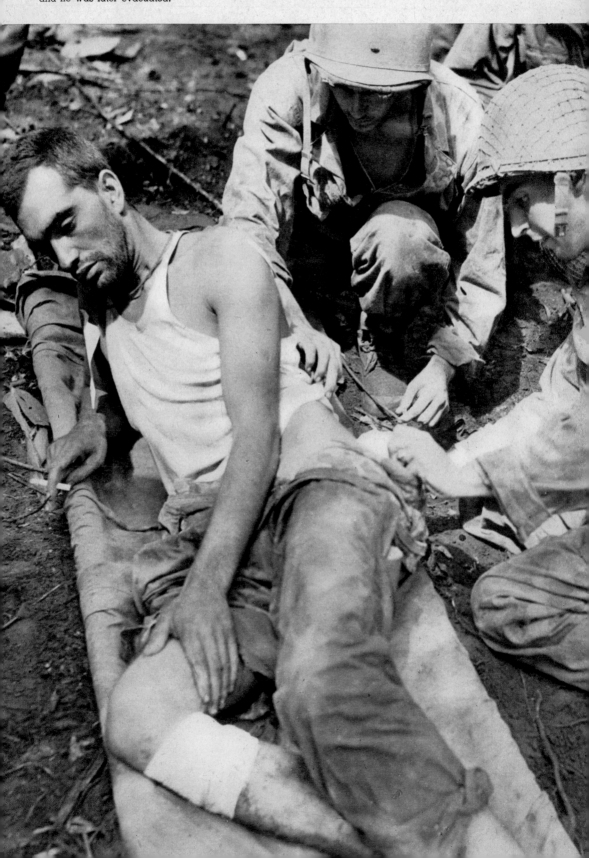

122. ...at Guadalcanal ...Russell ...Buna ... Woodlark...

Native stretcher bearers in New Guinea resting in a coconut grove while carrying American wounded from the front lines near Buna to hospitals.

123. ...at Munda ...the Trobriands ...Rendova ...Finschhafen...

Casualties aboard a lighter at Munda point, New Georgia.

124. ... at Kolombangara ... Koboda ... Salamaua ... Lae.

Native carriers, on the way back from a New Guinea battle, pause long enough for a wounded man to get a light from a member of the Medical Corps.

125. Wherever they go, American soldiers are accompanied by their faithful Medics, bearing whole "hospitals" on their backs.

A hospital unit hikes to the front after landing from a transport plane in New Guinea.

126. With them are some of the most skilled surgeons of the American medical profession, wearing khaki or dungarees for the duration.

Col. George A. Enion, a surgeon, observes a medical officer giving a surgical redressing to a casualty from bomb fragments. New Georgia.

127. In no war have the wounded had more capable and effective care. Evacuations are speeded by the best means available—sometimes by muleback...

In New Guinea, mechanization has not succeeded in replacing the army mule. Here, Pvt. Herman Jamnicke, of Tucson, Ariz., leads the animal while Sgt. John W. Nalson, also of Tucson, steadies the litter to prevent excessive rocking.

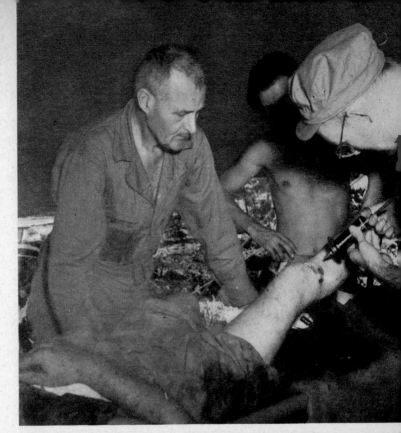

128. ... sometimes by jeep...

A Medical Corps unit in action in New Georgia. Note the mud-caked skid chains on the jeep's wheels. Chains are an absolute necessity in this region.

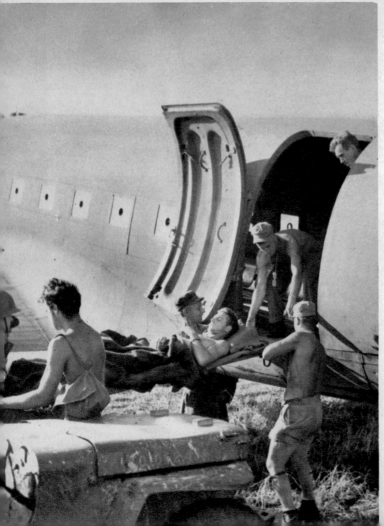

129. ... where possible, by plane...

A transport plane evacuates the wounded in New Guinea.

130. ... and eventually by hospital ship.

American and Australian soldiers in New Guinea board a hospital ship which will take them to Australia for further treatment and convalescence.

131. American nurses, who, on Bataan and Corregidor, added a glorious chapter to the history of women's courage ...

U. S. Army nurses waiting to disembark from a hospital ship somewhere in New Guinea.

132. ... follow the fighters wherever they go, getting as close to the firing lines as they are allowed.

After disembarking, the nurses pile into a "GI" truck to be taken to their new base.

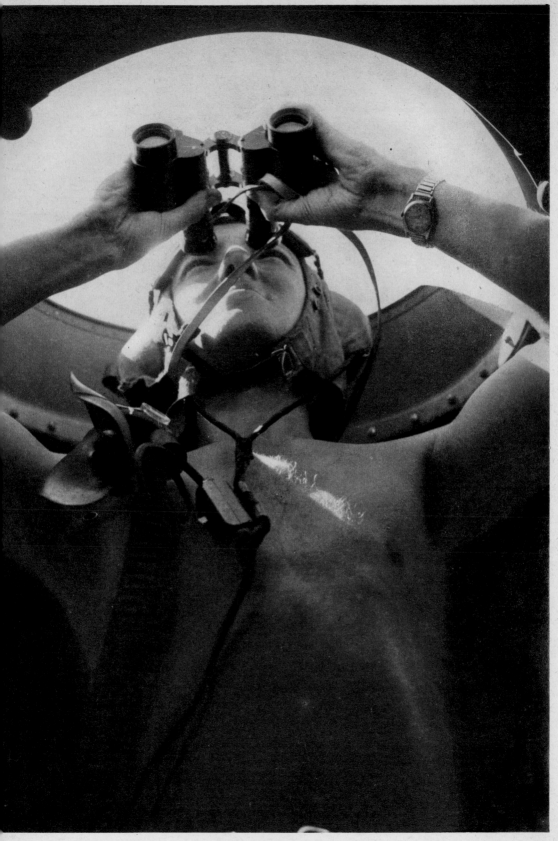

133. And while the infantryman slogs through the jungle marshes, the men of the air keep on the alert for Jap fliers.

A lookout in the observer's pit of a Lockheed Hudson bomber on patrol duty over the Solomon Islands.

134. The fields from which our airmen operate had to be hacked out of the jungle . . .

Natives help clear the ground.

135. . . . and made ready for smooth operation in record time.

Engineers lay portable strips for the runway.

136. Like men in love, our airmen call their ships anything from "Ecstasy" ...

Members of this transport crew carried supplies to Allied ground troops in New Guinea. Left to right: unidentified; Lt. Vernor L. Shea, pilot, San Francisco; Sgt. Ben F. Mortenson, engineer, Los Angeles; and Pfc. J. W. Hager, mechanic, Davidson, N. C.

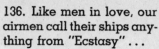

137. ... to "Gruesome."

Another crew of an advance echelon which brought supplies to our fighting forces in New Guinea. Left to right: Lt. Gene R. Glotzbach, pilot, Plainesville, Kan.; Lt. Henry W. Sherman, pilot, New York; Pfc. Marcellus A. Lamke, engineer, Aviston, Ill.; and Pfc. James A. Chapman, radio operator, West Frankport, Ill.

138. An amazing story of this war is how planes of the Troop Carrier Command flew an entire army division from Australia over the Owen Stanley Mountains . . .

The troop carriers in flight, photographed from one of their squadron. From Australia to New Guinea, they flew literally everything that an entire Army division would need: malaria pills, jeeps, road tractors, ammunition, guns, hospital units, food, a never-ending list of supplies, and —primarily—troops. Many of the troops fought in such dense and isolated country that the only contact possible was by air.

139. . . . to an otherwise inaccessible spot in New Guinea.

Curious natives come to stare at the monstrous mechanical bird which brought men and supplies to the battlefront.

140. Our bombers never cease to pound the enemy's airbases...

This remarkable picture was taken over Lae, New Guinea. A U. S. pilot, flying an A-20 plane approximately 100 feet above ground, strafes a number of Jap planes, including the disabled Jap bomber below and to left of it. At lower right is the remains of a Jap Zero. Another Zero lies damaged at the edge of the clearing at upper right. Two more Jap planes, torn by withering machine gun fire, are obscured by vegetation and trees at top center. The score this time was 5 to 0, in favor of the U. S. Army Air Forces.

141. ... until those bases are captured by our forces.

This plane, once part of Japan's air power, was blasted on the ground by U. S. bombers at Munda airfield on New Georgia Island. It now serves as an improvised clothesline for American soldiers occupying Munda.

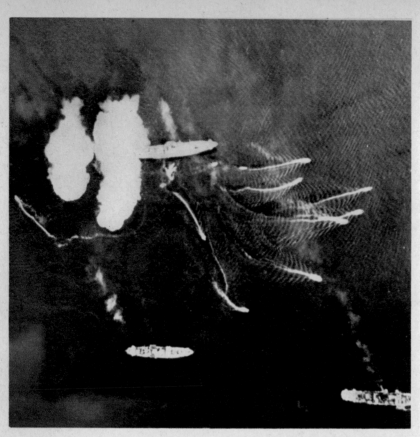

142. They played an im-portant role in the battle for Guadalcanal.

This Jap transport was trying to reinforce Japanese troops on Guadalcanal when it caught a direct hit from USAAF bombers. Landing barges scurry away from the flaming ship like so many tadpoles.

143. They fought off en-emy aircraft, and by April 1943 were shoot-ing down 7 Jap planes for every American plane lost.

Jap flying boat downed and sinking at Guadal-canal, its fuel flaming on the sea, at right.

44. On one day—June 16, 1943—U. S. fliers shot down 7 Jap planes over Guadalcanal, while losing only of their own.

Part of the spoils: a Jap Zero, its fuselage perforated, its wing shattered, its Rising Sun almost blasted away, by American marksmen.

45. Americans were quick to catch on to the enemy's tricks...

Jap transport, camouflaged to look like an island, is hit by an American bomb and begins to burn.

146. . . . and to give him back better than he sent.

On Oct. 12, 1943, bombers of the U. S. Army 5th Air Force blasted the Jap base at Rabaul, New Britain, where for months past the enemy had been concentrating reinforcements of men, planes, and equipment. More than 200 Jap craft were destroyed or damaged in this raid, in addition to other materiel, ships, and installations. This photo shows parachute bombs floating down on Vunakanau Airfield at Rabaul. Parachute bombs are used in low-altitude bombing to keep the attacking planes from being destroyed by their own bomb blasts. Note the Jap plane nosed into the ditch at lower left, and other enemy planes dispersed over the field and protected by revetments.

147. Japanese shipping has taken an incessant pounding from our bombers and fighters...

Jap merchant vessel afire from a bomb hit, with more bombs on the way, in lower right. Small boats are trying to pull away from the stricken ship. The water is covered with oil slicks.

148. ...and the enemy has often been forced to utilize barges to supply his island outposts.

Despite camouflage of boughs and branches which blends into the dense tropical foliage, this armada of loaded barges is spotted in a hide-out at Borgen Bay on the north coast of New Guinea. The 5th Air Force begins to bomb and strafe them, and within ten days 200 enemy barges are destroyed or rendered useless.

149. And remember what happened in the Battle of the Bismarck Sea!

A near miss off the port bow of this Jap destroyer, probably of the Sigure class. The undercarriage of the attacking plane is visible at top.

150. During that battle Lt. Gen. George Kenny's airmen killed more of the enemy ...

A B-25 sweeps in over the target to drop its bombs.

151. . . . than had been lost in any other great naval action in history.

This photo shows the result. The enemy destroyer has been rendered helpless, and another bomb, at right, is just about to strike and finish her off.

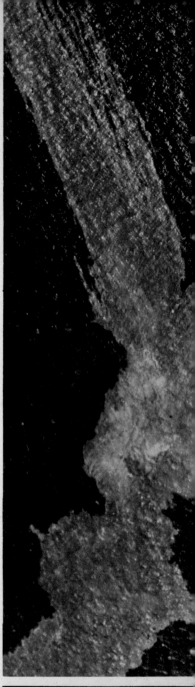

152. In that one engagement, American combat pilots completely wiped out a Jap fleet of 22 ships—12 troop transports and 10 cruisers and destroyers.

At sunset, during the Battle of the Bismarck Sea, an enemy destroyer, already crippled, tries to dodge a new attack, leaving a long oil slick in her wake, but American bombs find their mark.

153. For the 15,000 Jap lives lost in that battle, America lost only 13 men.

The battle continues after nightfall, with this attack on one of the enemy troopships. Four more bombs, center, are on the way.

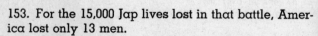

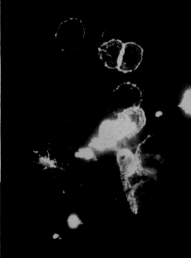

154. For the 52 Jap planes shot down and the 34 more probables, America gave up 4.

While attempting to refuel during the Battle of the Bismarck Sea, two Zeros are caught on the ground and set afire at Lae, New Guinea.

155. Back into Burma, out of whose jungles Gen. Stilwell had come painfully limping . . .

The U. S. 10th Air Force blasts a railway viaduct between Mandalay and the old Burma Road, rendering this important route useless to the enemy.

156. . . . roared the bombers of the USAAF to destroy Jap communications and installations with "pin-point" accuracy.

Minbu, a strategic Jap stronghold on the Irrawaddy River in central Burma, is visited by a bombing mission composed of B-24 Liberators.

157, 158, and 159. ... such as this Jap-operated cotton and cotton-seed oil plant at Allanmyo, Burma.

Before: The mill photographed when it was working full time, turning out its products for Nipponese military purposes. Key to photo: A—living quarters, B—warehouses, C—boiler house, D—ginning factory, E—unginned cotton, F—ground nut mill, G—workshops, H—pump house.

During: American bombs blanket the target, with direct hits on warehouses, workshops, ginning factory, and pump house.

After: Mission accomplished. In official language, the mill is now unserviceable. It was hit by 25 tons of bombs.

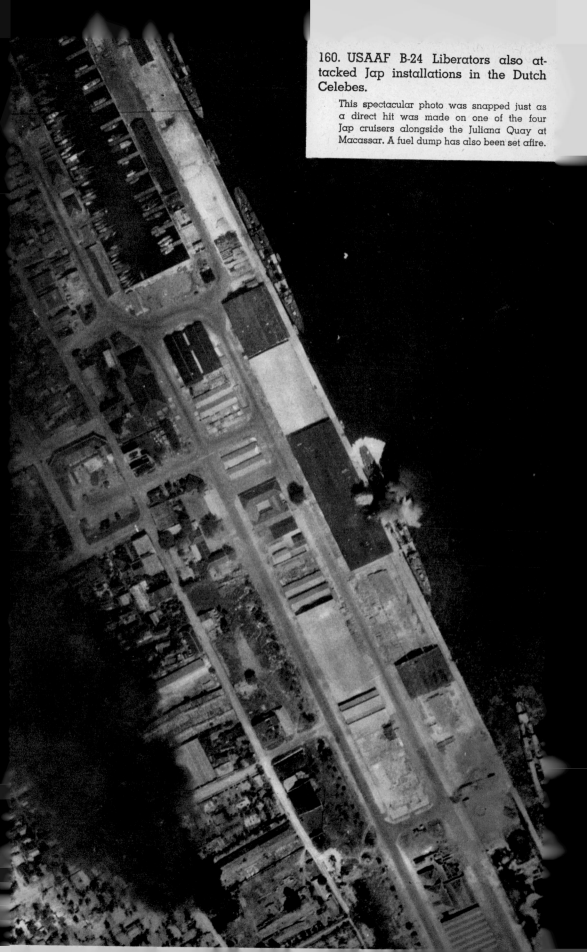

160. USAAF B-24 Liberators also attacked Jap installations in the Dutch Celebes.

This spectacular photo was snapped just as a direct hit was made on one of the four Jap cruisers alongside the Juliana Quay at Macassar. A fuel dump has also been set afire.

161. Anything short of pin-point accuracy would have failed on many a job that had to be done.

In spite of the extreme narrowness of the isthmus on which Salamaua is situated, American bombers hit it regularly, paving the way for the fall of this major Jap base on the north coast of New Guinea.

52. After Salamaua and Lae were captured by the Allies . . .

Bombs exploding on the airfield at Lae, New Guinea just before the Japs were driven out. Buildings at right are demolished. A direct hit is scored on the plane at left of center, which is burning. Airplanes in the dispersal area off the runway, including the bomber at lower left, have been damaged beyond repair.

53. . . . the Japs at Rabaul and Wewak began to hear regularly from our bombers.

Daring low-altitude flying by bombers of the USAAF sank many ships in this surprise raid on Wewak harbor. Here, a medium bomber, dodging bursts of anti-aircraft fire, has just dropped its bomb load beside a Jap freighter lying at anchor.

164. There was a hint of things to come . . .

These four action shots tell the dramatic story of our first use of paratroops in the Pacific. The Australians have already landed east of Lae and are attacking the 20,000 Japs there, whose route of escape is here, in the Markham Valley west of Lae. As General Douglas MacArthur watches from his plane, Boston bombers lay down this smokescreen along the Markham River.

165. A few minutes later these transports arrive on the scene. Behind the smokescreen American paratroopers begin to bail out, jumping from a lower altitude than has ever before been attempted in battle.

166. . . . in the way we took Lae.

A close-up of what is now happening simultaneously all over the valley. From right to left: the man closest to the plane has just jumped; the unopened parachute of the second man can be seen clear of his body; the third soldier's parachute has just opened, but is not yet fully inflated; the fourth is still swinging at an extreme angle from the initial shock of the parachute's opening; the fifth paratrooper is floating to the ground; and the sixth is preparing for his landing.

167. American paratroops are now sown thickly along the Markham River, the smokescreen still concealing their action from the Japs across the river. Many troops are still in the air. Others, already hidden by 12-foot-high pit-pit grass in the valley, are springing into action to cut off the Japs as Australians close in from the east.

168. Summing up our gains in the Pacific since Pearl Harbor, President Roosevelt said on Sept. 17, 1943: . . .

American troops landing supplies on one of our new island bases in the Pacific.

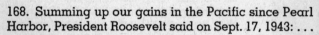

169. "American, Australian, New Zealand, and Dutch forces . . . have destroyed much Japanese strength . . .

A Bristol Beaufighter of the Royal Australian Air Forces passes a mountain peak en route to strafe Japanese military installations around Finschhafen harbor.

170. "... and have gained for us new bases from which to launch new offensive operations. ...

An American gun crew in New Guinea.

171. "... We have gained so many island air bases that the threat to Australia and New Zealand ... has been practically dissipated. ...

U. S. Army bombers leave their new base on a mission against the Japs.

172. "... In fact, it is safe to say that our position in that area has become a threat on our part against the Japanese. ...

USAAF B-24 Liberator bombers deliver their loads on a Japanese base in northern New Guinea. Direct hits are made on shoreline installations, and smoke rises thousands of feet, higher than the attacking planes themselves.

173. "... The Japanese hold firmly established positions on an enormous front from the Kuriles through the mandated islands to the Solomons, and through the Netherlands East Indies to Malaysia and Burma and China....

On Nov. 2, 1943, American B-25 medium bombers raid the enemy's major base at Rabaul, destroying harbor installations, sinking 15 Jap ships, and damaging 11 more. The harbor, according to Gen. MacArthur's communique, is "practically swept clean."

174. "... To break through this defensive ring, we must hit them and hit them hard, not merely at one point, but at many points, and we must keep on hitting them."

A Jap casualty on the beach near Buna Mission.

II

THE CAMPAIGN IN THE ALEUTIANS

IN THE seventh month of war with Japan our Aleutian outposts were attacked and invaded. On June 4, 1942, following an enemy bomber attack on Dutch Harbor, 2,547 miles east of Yokohama, our Army and Navy fliers located a Jap fleet of at least 2 carriers, 2 cruisers, and 8 destroyers, 165 miles to the southwest. Despite fog, rain, and unfavorable weather, our aircraft, in repeated attacks, sank 1 enemy cruiser, damaged another, and forced the Japanese to withdraw. Nevertheless, 10 days later, a hostile task force of cruisers and transports was discovered at Kiska Island. Attu, where the International Date Line swerves sharply to encompass our westernmost point in the Aleutians, was also discovered to have been occupied by the enemy.

Strategically, the occupation of these barren islands was of comparatively small importance, as General George C. Marshall, U. S. Army Chief of Staff, has pointed out. There was, however, the possibility of infiltrations along the island chain which might eventually permit the enemy to operate against our sea routes along the southwestern coast of Alaska. The occupation had a strong psychological effect, particularly among residents in the Pacific northwest. Estimates were made that 10,000 Japanese troops had taken up positions in the Aleutians.

No immediate measures were taken to recapture these positions, because of the lack of ships, planes, and trained troops.

But within three months of highly concentrated effort the necessary supplies, weapons, ships, planes, and personnel were assembled for an initial landing on Adak in the Andreanof Islands, some 200 miles to the east of Jap-held Kiska. The occupation was effected by our forces on August 31, 1942 without opposition from the enemy.

From Adak, Army bombers flew through fog, snow, and subzero weather to pound incessantly the entrenched Japs on Kiska and Attu. Navy task forces bombarded the enemy from offshore. The first mass raid against Kiska was launched Sept. 14, 1942. Soon destroyed were the enemy air forces, and attempts to reinforce their garrison were checked by destruction of their shipping en route to Kiska.

Complete encirclement of the Japanese on Kiska now accomplished, our first land engagement with the enemy began in a heavy fog on the morning of May 11, 1943, when a task force composed of a portion of the 7th Infantry Division, reinforced, landed on Attu, heavily supported by its naval escort. This was warfare under the most rugged conditions imaginable. The fighting was over mountainous terrain in deep snows and thick fog. On May 31, the operation was successfully completed with the annihilation of 2,350 Japanese. Only 24 prisoners were taken. Five hundred and twelve American soldiers were lost.

The backbone of Jap resistance was now broken. When a U. S. landing force came ashore at Quisling Cove on the western coast of Kiska, August 15, 1943, not a living Jap could be found. Some time previous the enemy had evacuated the garrison, though U. S. Army Air Forces combat camera views taken during an attack showed them cowering in anti-aircraft artillery revetments.

Thus in 14 months the Jap and his threat to our northernmost possessions had vanished. In regaining the Aleutians we also came into possession of air fields, underground passages, and supply dumps which the enemy had energetically constructed, and which are now employed in our defense of the islands.

DISTANCES IN STATUTE MI
Attu to Kiska....................
Attu to Amchitka...............
Attu to Cape Lopatka..........
Attu to Tokyo....................
Kiska to Amchitka.............
Kiska to Dutch Harbor........

Area held by Japa

ATTU I.

Miles
0 5 10

Kresta Point
Red Head
Stellar Cove
Cape Wrangell
3084
Holtz Bay
U. S. FORCES
Attu Village
Chichagof Ha
C. Klebiko
Sarana Ba
Abraham Pt.
Abraham Bay
Nevidiskov Bay
Temna Bay
U. S. FORCES
Massacre Bay
Theodore Pt.

ARCTIC OCEAN

WRANGELL I.

Chuniksak Pt.

Arctic   Circle

S.   R.

ALASKA
Nome
Anchorage
KODIAK I.

Bering Str.
ST. LAWRENCE I.
60°

SEA OF KHOTSK

Kamchatka Peninsula

BERING   SEA

Alaska Pen.

UNIMAK I.

KOMANDORSKIE IS.

Date
Line

International

PRIBILOF IS.

Dutch Harbor
UNALASKA I.
UMNAK I.
FOX IS.

50°

Petropavlovsk

SEGUAM
AMLIA
ATKA
KANAGA
TANAGA
ATTU I.
AGATTU
KISKA
RAT
AMCHITKA
ADAK
ANDREANOF IS.
NEAR IS.
RAT IS.

Paramushiru
C. Lopatka

ISLANDS

ALEUTIAN   ISLANDS

40°

NORTH   PACIFIC   OCEAN

160°   170°   180°   170°   40°

175. Nips in the Aleutians! To blast them out America needed bases in Alaska...

Freight being unloaded from ships in Skagway Harbor for transportation on the White Pass & Yukon Railroad to Whitehorse, Yukon Territory.

176. ... and ships, men, and guns.

A 155mm. gun is lowered into a landing barge off the coast of Alaska.

177. Supplies were moved by the most modern method...
Unloading a cargo transport on an Alaskan airfield. The tanks contain oxygen for high-altitude flying.

178. ...as well as the most primitive...
Soldiers haul their gun up an Alaskan mountain pass.

79. . . . through snow and everlasting mud . . .
A work detail plows through the Alaskan mud, taking it in good spirits.

80. . . . but they *got there*.
Water and food supplies in a dump area on one of our new island bases not far from Jap-held Kiska.

181. Rivaling the legendary feats of Paul Bunyan, Army engineers pierced the Canadian wilds to build ...

Two huge tractors grading for construction of the roadbed in northern Canada.

182. ... the 1600-mile Alca[n] Highway to Alaska in an amaz[z]ingly short time.

A convoy of trucks moves supplies over the new road.

183. Before Americans could face the Japs with cold steel ...

A jeep comes ashore and gets stuck in the Alaskan mud.

184. ... they had to take cold, foggy beaches ...

Rucksacks are unloaded on an Alaskan beach. In background, other barges from the convoy approach shore.

185. . . . and transform forbidding marshland . . .

Bulldozers clear sand from bottom of this bay inlet to enable engineers to lay an airfield. The sand is pushed to the field, where it is used to fill in soft spots.

186. . . . into efficient airfields.

A P-40 ready to take off from one of the new Alaskan airfields. The sea of mud surrounding the taxiway gives some indication of the difficulties encountered.

. And they had to
d many other things,
at . . .

Hangar being built by Air
Corps Engineers.

188. . . . and small. →

189. This cold, forbidding land developed . . .

190. . . . a type of American soldier . . .

191. . . . wor

193. . . . always ready for fun . . .

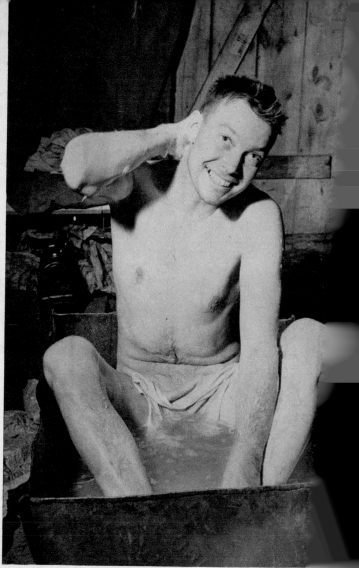

frontier ancestors ...

192. ... men who were adaptable ...

194. . . . tough in body . . .

195. . . . steadfast in faith.

196. Suddenly the drive was on!
A heavy weapons unit on the march.

197. On Aug. 31, 1942, Americans landed on Adak in the Andreanofs . . .

On the second day after their arrival, the beach was crowded with equipment and rations, which were quickly removed to sheltered sections. This 37mm. rapid-fire anti-aircraft gun was one of many set up on the beach.

198. ... first stepping stone ...

A staff sergeant, with tent pitched on Adak Island, is cleaning up, ready for anything.

200. After two weeks of hard work ...

Tired members of the beach gang snatch a few minutes sleep beside ration boxes they have just unloaded in the And

199. . . . between
Alaska and Attu.

A machine-gun—
one of many—is set
up to guard our
new outpost.

201. . . . our new base on Adak was ready . . .

An anti-aircraft gun crew on the alert for Jap planes that may
come out of the fog.

202. . . . to launch the first mass air raid on the Japs at Kiska.

In their warm hut, pilots and navigators relax before taking off to bomb Kiska.

203. The airmen gathered in the briefing room for their instructions.

Wide-awake now, and serious faced, pilots listen to Maj. Milton Askins before their flight over Kiska.

204. Out came the bombs . . .

205. . . . in went the bullets.

206. One last word and they were o[ff]
Bombers bound for Kiska gather around C[olonel]
William O. Eareckson before the take-off.

207. Zooming out of the Aleutian mis[t]
they came in over Kiska. Bombs away

208. ...and it's a hit! One of many hits — on one of many days.

209. Back home they came, ready to do it again tomorrow —and tomorrow.

When this picture was taken, Capt. George Laven, Jr., of San Antonio, Tex., had 2 Zeros to his credit, and Lt. Stanley Long of Marquette, Mich., had downed a 4-motored bomber.

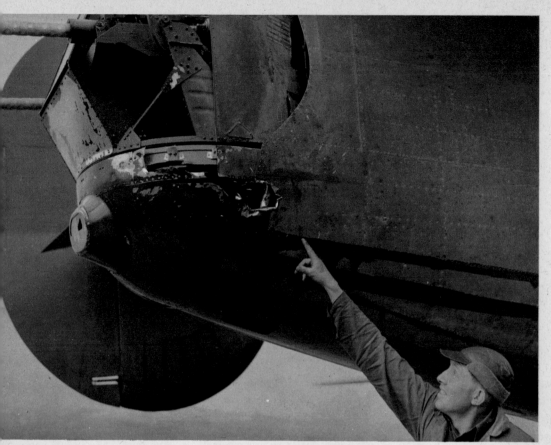

210. And how did the ship come through?

Donald L. Mitchell of Birdseye, Utah, points to the tail turret of a Consolidated B-25, damaged by anti-aircraft fire.

211. There'll be a patch needed here...

Lt. John J. Brahan of Long Beach, N. Y., remembers a close call as he examines a shrapnel hole in the nose of his Consolidated B-24 after a raid on Kiska. The Japs didn't just sit and take it.

212. . . . the belly guns need cleaning . . .

Mechanics working on a B-17E after its return from Kiska. One man is cleaning the barrel of a machine gun while the other two are working on the belly turret.

213. . . . and the turret guns . . .
Sgt. Wm. M. Paret of Flushing, N. Y.

214. . . . and the windows.
Sgt. Dick Hazelhurst of Peoria, Ill.
astride a North American B-25.

**215. Now to cover up the
wings and put her to bed—
until the next run.**
A North American B-25.

216. Gen. George C. Marshall reported: "The Japanese air forces in the Kiska region were soon destroyed ...

Maj. Gen. William O. Butler, commanding 11th U. S. Air Force, awards Air Medal to Capt. Morgan A. Giffin of San Antonio, Tex., "somewhere in the Andreanofs."

217. "... and his attempts to reinforce the garrison were rendered relatively ineffective by the destruction of his shipping en route to Kiska."

USAAF bombers literally blew this 280-foot Jap patrol boat out of the water at a harbor in the Aleutians. As the camera recorded this action the after part of the vessel was hidden by multiple explosions. A few seconds later, the ship rose from the water and snapped apart.

218. But we needed bases still farther west. So on Jan. 12, 1943 ...

Landing operations during occupation of Amchitka Island by a U. S. Army task force.

219. . . . an American task force landed unopposed on Amchitka.

220. "In the late spring," Gen. Marshall reported, "shipping and material, though limited, at last became available . . .

The enemy stronghold at Chichagof Harbor, Attu Island. Smoke at shoreline is from burning Jap installations bombed by USAAF.

...hese troops coming ashore on Amchitka are only 69 miles from the Japs on Kiska.

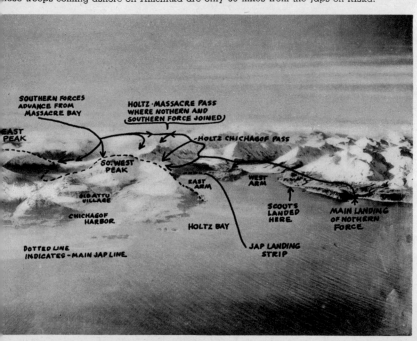

SOUTHERN FORCES ADVANCE FROM MASSACRE BAY

HOLTZ·MASSACRE PASS WHERE NOTHERN AND SOUTHERN FORCE JOINED

EAST PEAK

HOLTZ CHICHAGOF PASS

SO. WEST PEAK

OLD ATTU VILLAGE

EAST ARM

WEST ARM

CHICHAGOF HARBOR

HOLTZ BAY

SCOUTS LANDED HERE

MAIN LANDING OF NOTHERN FORCE

DOTTED LINE INDICATES - MAIN JAP LINE

JAP LANDING STRIP

221. "... to launch a formal challenge to the enemy's occupation of the Aleutians ...

Aerial view of the northern side of Attu Island. American scouts were landed on ridge at right to screen the main American landing, which was made farther right at Red Beach. Other American forces landed on the south side of the island and advanced from Massacre Bay.

222. "... A task force composed of a portion of the 7th Infantry Division, reinforced, ...

American troops swarm ashore at Red Beach, Attu.

223. "... landed on Attu Island, the outermost island of the Aleutian chain, on the morning of May 11, 1943, heavily supported by its naval escort ...

Landing boats shuttle back and forth between troop transports and the rugged shore.

224. "... Heavy fogs limited air action ...

Thirty yards in from the beach, bottomless mud made it impossible to use any heavy vehicles. Here a bulldozer is bogged down, its broad treads almost completely buried.

225. "... Despite the mountainous character of the country, deep snow, and the absence of roads, ...

Because of the mud, this 37 mm. anti-tank gun, as well as all artillery used, had to be hauled into position by hand.

226. "...the troops...fought their way across the island ..."

Americans seize the ridge between Red Beach and Holtz Bay, and pockmark the tundra with innumerable foxholes.

227. "... to encircle the Japanese troops defending Chichagof Harbor ...

Battle for a mountain pass leading into Chichagof Harbor. U. S. troops, at left, are moving toward Jap positions in the valley. Japs also have gun positions just above fog line.

228. "... There on May 31 the operation ...

At Massacre Bay, an 81 mm. mortar fires into a Jap-held valley. The soldier with telephone is receiving firing data from a forward observer.

229. "... was successfully ...

Battle above Massacre Bay. U. S. Infantry are advancing under fire across a low area toward bitterly-defended Jap positions on the ridge to right of snow circle which resembles the Rising Sun. Dark spots are Japanese gun emplacements and openings to underground barracks.

230. "... terminated ...

Japanese soldiers killed during the battle at Holtz I

... after a loss of 512 American sol-
...

bodies of 5 Americans, killed in the battle at
z Bay, have just been evacuated from the front
are awaiting proper burial. Under each body is
oard to which the soldier's identification tag has
n attached.

232. "... against the annihilation of 2,350
Japanese ...

Rather than surrender, these Japanese soldiers pulled
the pins of their own grenades and held them against
their bodies. The picture shows them just as they fell.
The Aleutian campaign also cost the enemy 9 to 13
men-of-war sunk and 16 others damaged, plus 30 non-
combat vessels sunk or damaged.

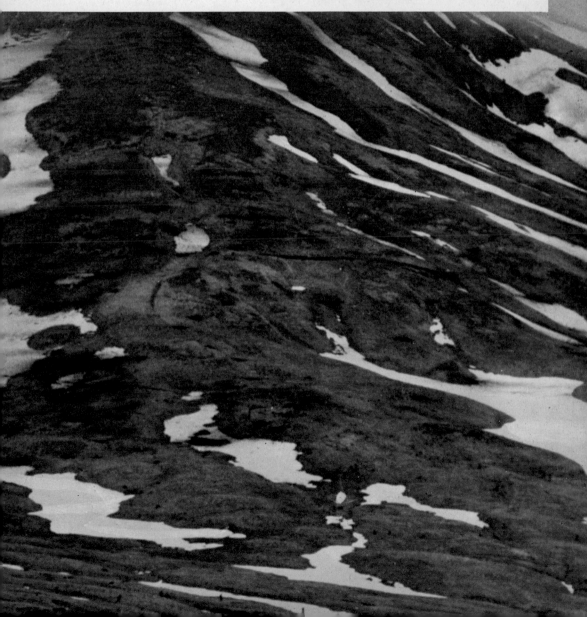

233. "...The capture of Attu evidently came as a complete surprise to the enemy ..."

On the beach of Holtz Bay, the Japanese had installed a battery of 6 duo-purpose anti-aircraft and field artillery guns, but because of the speed of the American attack, the enemy was prevented from disabling these guns when they retreated. In consequence, U. S. forces turned the weapons against their former owners. The tunnel entrance at right leads to an underground Jap barracks, which, in turn, is connected to the next gun of the battery.

S.E. END OF RUNWAY

234. "...who had anticipated an assault on Kiska...

Shortly before Chichagof Bay was taken by our forces, the Japanese there, realizing that they were doomed, organized a final suicide raid on the American lines. The commander of the troops issued an order that any man who could not participate in the raid was to be killed. This order was carried out so thoroughly that even the wounded Japanese soldiers in the field hospital were slain by their own officers, and the building was then set afire. This still-smoking shambles is what the Americans found when they arrived on the scene.

235. "...which now lay trapped by our planes and naval craft."

With the fall of Attu, American airmen concentrated their attention on the enemy's last remaining stronghold in the Aleutians. This aerial photograph shows the Jap's laboriously constructed airfield at Kiska during one of our raids. "AA" marks enemy anti-aircraft positions. These are connected by communicating trenches, one of which, in center, has just received a direct hit. Smoke columns in background indicate other Jap installations damaged.

236. Kiska's turn was next.

Etched on a sunlit sea, ships of the U. S. Navy ride at anchor in the harbor of an Aleutian island base, just before the push on Kiska. This picture was made by a U. S. Navy photographer from a Vega Ventura bomber patrolling the skies over the invasion armada.

On Aug. 15, 1943, Ameri-
and Canadian forces land-
...

roops wading ashore from their
nding craft at Broad Beach, Kiska.

238. . . . but they met no Japs.

Landing barges back away after discharging their initial loads.

239. The enemy had fled!

Jap anti-aircraft guns had fired at us only 2 days before our troops landed. Among abandoned Jap supplies our men found raw meat in good condition and canned milk that was still sweet, which may indicate that some Japs were making their escape at other points even while we were landing. But in their haste to get away they took time out to scribble this greeting on the wall of their former headquarters on Kiska.

240. The Aleutian Campaign was now successfully finished.

With the planting of the Canadian and American flags on Kiska, the enemy's North Pacific front had been pushed back some 1,000 miles nearer Japan—to Paramushiru, where it had been on Dec. 7, 1941. The sentry in this picture is Pvt. James L. Penton of Shoshone, Wyo.

III

THE MEDITERRANEAN CAMPAIGN

IN THE summer of 1942, the army of German Field Marshal Rommel had pushed to within 70 miles of Alexandria, menacing Egypt and the entire Middle East. Axis air power had cut the Mediterranean in two, and battered Allied convoys were barely keeping alive the defense of Malta. Supplies and reinforcements for the British army in Egypt had to go around the Cape of Good Hope. Yet in these desperate days, Allied leaders laid plans not only for defense but for victory; plans to drive the Axis out of Africa, to reopen the Mediterranean, and to expose "the underbelly" of Europe to attack.

Every resource was strained to send men, tanks, and planes to the British army in Egypt. Simultaneously, and in the utmost secrecy, a vast sea-borne expedition to Morocco and Algeria was prepared. A hundred thousand men, British and American, were trained and equipped for desert warfare, were supplied with armor and airplanes. Successful negotiations for French cooperation were quietly carried on.

The first blow was struck by General Montgomery on Oct. 23, at El Alamein, where Rommel's army was shattered and driven in headlong flight. Before dawn on Nov. 8, combined British and American forces under General Eisenhower landed near Casablanca, Oran, and Algiers in French North Africa. Surprise was complete, and French resistance soon turned to cooperation. Allied forces were rushed eastward toward Tunis, but 30 miles outside that city they were stopped by German troops and armor ferried over from Europe by plane and ship, for Axis air power still dominated the Sicilian strait.

Throughout the winter, mud-bound armies in Tunisia exchanged indecisive blows, but in the drier south, Montgomery's veteran 8th Army relentlessly drove Rommel westward along more than 1,400 miles of coast. At the Mareth line in southern

Tunisia, Rommel made a stand, but Montgomery, supported by overwhelming air power, hammered him northward. By April 20, Axis forces were penned in northern Tunisia, and the Allies, under General Eisenhower as Allied Supreme Commander, opened a final crushing offensive. British, American, and French forces smashed steadily forward from all sides until, on May 6, the last Axis defensive ring around Tunis and Bizerte was cut into isolated segments. Unable to escape by sea or air, 252,415 Germans and Italians surrendered. Africa and the Mediterranean were freed.

Between Tunis and Italy lay two island strongholds, Pantelleria and Sicily. The first was subdued by a few days of terrific bombing from the air, symbolic of the air ascendancy which the Allies kept throughout the year, but Sicily called for bloodier work. On July 10, the British 8th Army got a foothold on the southeast corner and drove northward toward Catania. Simultaneously, the American 7th Army landed on the southern coast and fought its way clear across the island to Palermo, then turned east to join the British in cornering the German and Italian forces

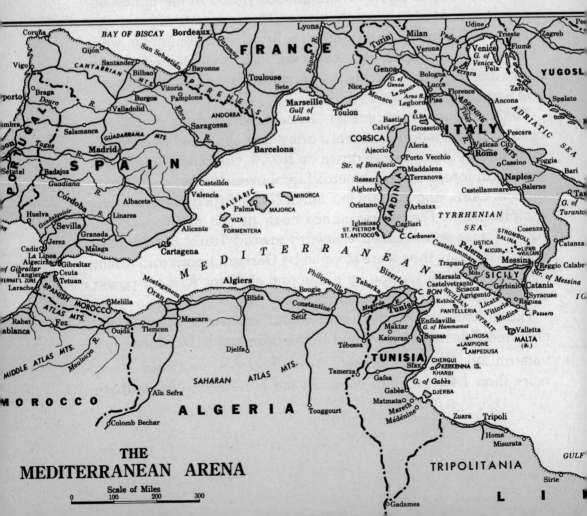

THE
MEDITERRANEAN ARENA

Scale of Miles
0   100   200   300

between Mt. Etna and Messina. Under terrific pressure by land, sea, and air, the enemy slowly gave ground and 38 days after the landing, the island was conquered.

Sicily was only a stepping-stone to the continent of Europe. On Sept. 3, 8th Army units landed on the toe of Italy and found resistance weak. Accumulated Fascist military disasters led to anti-Fascist revolution and on Sept. 8, General Eisenhower announced the unconditional surrender of the Italian government. On the next day, General Clark's 5th Army seized a perilous bridgehead near Salerno in the face of fierce German resistance. By the 17th, this bridgehead was secure, and contact was established with Montgomery, whose forces swept through Taranto to Brindisi and Bari on the Adriatic Sea, and on to the great air base at Foggia. On Oct. 1, Naples fell to the 5th Army, but, just beyond, the Germans made a determined stand on a strong line behind the Volturno River and stretching thence right across the mountainous peninsula to the Adriatic.

By the end of October, those defenses had been forced in heavy fighting and the enemy was defending a new line a little farther north. Rain, snow, and the rugged Apennine Mountains were allies of the Germans, but unremitting pressure had forced them to throw in many veteran divisions. They seemed resolved to contest bitterly every foot of Italian soil in order to hold Rome as long as they could.

Thus in little more than a year after the beginning of the Mediterranean offensive, the Allies swept beyond North Africa to Sicily, Sardinia, Corsica, and the Continent. This campaign accomplished much. It took Italy out of the war. It encouraged resistance in Yugoslavia and Greece, threatening the Balkan communications of the Axis. It severely strained the entire German defensive system in southern Europe. It gained bases like Foggia, from which central and eastern Europe could be reached by effective bomber attack. The Allied push from El Alamein and Casablanca into Italy was indeed a long stride on the road to victory.

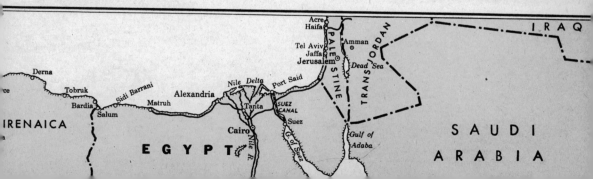

THE CAMPAIGN IN NORTH AFRICA

241. The Mediterranean story beg[an] quietly enough when, in the fall of 19[42] an American general left London for [an] unknown destination.

The man with the secret mission—Gen. M[ark] Clark, shown here with British officers. [He] carried out the hazardous assignment of la[nd]ing in French North Africa and persuad[ing] certain authorities there to cooperate with [the] Allies when the invasion came. "Not unt[il] days before the convoys would deploy off [the] beaches," said Gen. George C. Marsh[all,] "were the few Frenchmen we had contac[ted] informed of the actual date for the operatio[n."]

242. Headed for the same destination, and already on the high seas, were 3 huge task forces . . .

Five-inch gun on one of the ships in the convoy of U. S. troops en route to French Morocco during the first week of November, 1942. "The ships for such an amphibious operation," President Roosevelt later explained, "cannot be loaded in the ordinary way, to be unloaded alongside a comfortable, safe wharf. Most of the ships must be 'combat loaded' in such a way that the troops go ashore first and are immediately followed in the proper order by guns and ammunition, tanks, trucks and food, medical equipment and all the supplies of a modern army. Preparations must be made to conduct these landings under enemy fire, and on beaches instead of docks."

243. . . . comprising the greatest armada history had yet seen.

Part of the convoy. "Three task forces were formed: one entirely American sailed directly from the United States and carried out the landings along the west coast of Morocco; another of American troops escorted by the British Navy sailed from Great Britain and landed in the vicinity of Oran; the third, a combined British-American ground force escorted by the British Navy, sailed from the British Isles and landed at Algiers."—Gen. Marshall.

244. From the decks of each vessel, men peered at the sea, proud of their strength, sure of their cause.

U. S. troops en route to North Africa aboard the S.S. Dickman.

245. On the morning of Nov. 8, 1942, French North Africans awoke to find their coasts lined with Allied vessels. Men clambered over the rails . . .

Rangers descending into assault boats to participate in the capture of an Algerian harbor.

246. . . . and swung down the sides of their ships into invasion barges.

Each soldier carries a heavy load of equipment, yet both hands are free for action.

247. Under the guns of their fleet the barges swarmed toward shore.

Anti-aircraft crews protecting assault boats during landing operations at Fedala Harbor, French Morocco.

248. In each barge, as the waves slapped against the sides, the men had a few last moments to wonder about what might lie ahead of them.

249. Each man, whether he was from Tucson or Brooklyn, had been trained to be an expert on some particular strip of African beach . . .

Assault troops wading a-shore from landing barges.

250. ... and knew exactly what he had to do.

U. S. Rangers forcing the door of a questionable building during the early stage of the fighting for an Algerian harbor. Along the whole coast, the tactics were the same: landings above and below each city, the seizing of airports, railroads, lines of communication, then swift convergence upon the cities themselves.

251. The three task forces struck simultaneously at
Casablanca, Oran, and Algiers, and points of resistance
were bombarded by the fleet.

Guns on North Point, near Safi, French Morocco, shelled and put out of commission by the U. S. Navy.

252. "The landings were carried out," reported Gen. Marshall, "with a boldness and efficiency which secured the initial objectives ...

American troops in possession of a fort that had been shelled by the U. S. Navy. While similar operations were under way all along the coast, American paratroops and air-borne infantry flew in from the British Isles, 1,500 miles away, and captured the airports at Oran and Algiers.

253. "... the major airfields and ports in North Africa within a period of 48 hours."

An armored division of our infantry passing through Rabat, French Morocco.

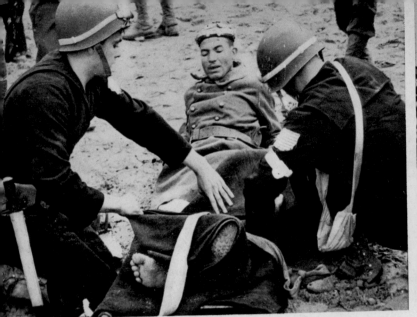

254. On Nov. 9, Vichy ordered French African units to resist our forces...

Americans administering first-aid to a French-African soldier.

256. ...except on the Casablanca front...

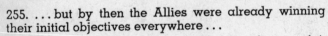

255. ...but by then the Allies were already winning their initial objectives everywhere...

U. S. soldiers in foxholes of a forward defense line near their landing beach.

French battleship, Jean Bart,
naged by U. S. shellfire in
sablanca harbor after it had
d on Allied forces.

257. . . . where the strongest opposition was encountered.
American soldiers in North Africa take up field positions.

258. In the early morning of Nov. 11, a few minutes before the
assault was to be launched on that city ...

An Italian merchant ship, damaged by the U. S. Navy at Casablanca, capsizes
at her pier.

59. . . . Admiral Darlan ordered all rench commanders in North Africa . . .

A French Moroccan harbor seen through a shellhole in a bombed building.

260. . . . to cease hostilities.

French officers who later led the Goums to victory against the Axis.

261. French North Africa joined the Allies, and . . .

The famous French-Arabian cavalry unit, the Algerian Spahis.

262. . . . once again American and French soldiers prepared to fight side by side.

An American soldier teaches a new French comrade how to fire a Garand rifle.

263. Lafayette would have been pleased.

264. The first phase of the Allied plan was now completed.

Gen. Henri Giraud and officers of his staff inspecting an M-4 tank sent from America for use by the French.

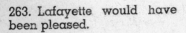

265. Meanwhile, from the east, came the rumble of Rommel's 1,700-mile retreat from El Alamein...

U. S. troops marching through a French Moroccan town.

266. . . . with Montgomery's British 8th Army at his heels.

Mountain outlook of a U. S. fighter group, with one of our new airfields in the valley below.

267. With new bases established for our land, sea, and air forces . . .

In a daylight attack, USAAF bombers raid the important Axis-held port of Tripoli, landing direct hits on a pierhead in the harbor. Note that Axis shipping crowds every available space at the pier, while 14 other vessels are anchored near by, awaiting their turn to unload supplies for Rommel's army.

268. . . . we were now ready for a pincer movement of our own.

American Rangers on the march in North Africa.

269. As quickly as logistic support could be prepared . . .

American sugar piled up in a quartermaster's depot at Casablanca.

271. . . . to exterminate the enemy in Africa.

German soldier shot and killed while trying to escape in his halftrack.

270. . . . the Allied forces closed in on Tunisia . . .

A Ranger battalion takes to the hills on a speed march.

272 Back of the lines, where American aid was revitalizing a
war-torn people . . .

Arabs examining lend-lease supplies.

273. . . . the Nazis did their best to upset our plans . . .

Searchlights over Algiers as Allied forces train anti-aircraft artillery and machine guns on raiding Nazi planes.

274. . . . by bombing the ports which had fallen into Allied hands.

Wreckage in Algiers after Axis raid on the night of Jan. 26, 1943.

275. One day in January, 1943, at Casablanca, doughboys stared with astonishment at the unexpected sight of their President.

Sgt. Oran Lass, of Kansas City, Mo., drives the President's jeep. Behind the President, Gen. Mark Clark now wears three stars on his cap.

276. While admirals and generals worked out the details . . .

High Army and Navy officials of Great Britain and the United States in discussion at the Casablanca Conference.

277. . . . the Allied leaders summed up their plans for the enemy in two words: "UNCONDITIONAL SURRENDER!"

On the lawn of the President's villa: Gen. Henri Honoré Giraud, President Roosevelt, Gen. Charles de Gaulle, and Prime Minister Churchill.

278. To accomplish this, British, French, and American troops und◄

U. S. armored unit passes a French garrison on the way to the front.

279. . . . closed in on the Axis forces in Tunisia from the east, south, and west.

Vanguard of an American tank column advancing across the desert to strengthen Allied positions.

mand of Gen. Dwight D. Eisenhower .

280. To the north, Allied naval and air forces concentrated on cutting the enemy's last supply rou
for a while Axis reinforcements continued to pour in and Rommel's resistance stiffened.

Huge American B-25 bombers fly low over their camp after taking off on a mission. Bombers like
these softened up Rommel's Mareth Line and played a large part in all operations against the
Afrika Korps.

281. On February 14, 1943, while these U. S. Army Waacs (now Wacs) paraded in Tri-Nation ceremonies in North Africa . . .

282. . . . enemy armored units, infantry, artillery, and air power struck westward from Faid and broke through Kasserine Pass.

Kasserine Pass as seen from a plane several miles above it. The clusters of dark spots that resemble trees are bursts of American bombs on Axis gun positions guarding the pass.

283. A week later, the enemy had thrust 21 miles beyond the pass and was making his last offensive effort in Tunisia . . .

Distant view of the German 10th Panzer Division, appearing as black dots, undergoing American artillery fire. There were considerable tank losses on both sides in the battle at Kasserine Pass.

284. ... before he recoiled under a concentrated attack, powerfully assisted by the entire Allied air force in North Africa.

Two German tanks, knocked out by American artillery, are burning in the distance. The soldier in foreground has dug himself a foxhole.

285. The Allies resume their interrupted advance by erasing many colorf names from the Axis ma of Africa ...

287. Ksar Rhilane ... Gafsa ... El Guettar.

...ld artillery crew loads a
...n. howitzer

286. ...Sbeitla...Nefta...Hallouf...
American "Long Toms" (155mm. rifles) register on positions
occupied by German artillery at El Guettar. In this battle the
enemy was repulsed with severe losses in men and tanks.

...n prisoners, 280 of them, are lined up to march to the rear of the Allied lines after their
...re 8 miles south of El Guettar.

288. The British stormed and took the Mareth Line.

Allied losses of equipment were not always total write-offs, as this picture shows. A strafed half-track and a shattered jeep are loaded on a tank transporter for evacuation to a railroad. From there they will go to Constantine, Algeria for salvage.

289. On April 7 a great moment came when patrols of the U. S. 2nd Corps, advancing southeast from Gafsa ...

A long line of Allied transports, on their way to the front with supplies for the advancing troops, passes what is left of an enemy encampment. The roofless buildings in the foreground, with bomb craters all around them, were formerly occupied by men of Rommel's army.

290. . . . made contact with units of the British 8th Army, 20 miles from the coast.

Greetings from the British 1st Army and the U. S. 2nd Corps to the British 8th Army on the occasion of their junction for a united drive on Axis forces.

291. With sudden might, Allied air power now seized . . .

North American B-25's of the Northwest African Air Force, which consisted of the U. S. 12th Air Force and some units of the RAF.

292. ...and maintained control...

Junk pile of fuselages, wings, and engine parts left behind by the enemy when they were forced to evacuate one of their airports in North Africa.

293. ...over the Axis in this theatre.

One of Rommel's supply trains after USAAF fighters had strafed it from the air. In aerial combat our fighters defeated and routed a force of German and Italian fighters which greatly outnumbered them.

294. In 14 days of attacks...

U. S. planes on their way to Axis-held territory from one of their new bomber bases in Algiers.

295. ...on airfields...

Derelict ME-110's bombed into uselessness on an Axis landing field. Similar evidence of the deadly accuracy of our bombardiers was found at every airfield taken by our forces. Hundreds of other planes, hastily abandoned as Rommel's men fled before our advance, fell into Allied hands almost undamaged.

296. . . . ports and . . .

Ferryville, near Bizerte, Tunisia, takes a pounding as Boeing B-17 Flying Fortresses unload their bombs on docks, ships, and oil tanks, scoring direct hits on a ship at the southern end of the main dock, damaging several others' in the harbor, and starting fires along the water front. This raid crippled installations on which the Germans depended to bring supplies by sea to their hard-pressed forces.

297. . . . communications between Sicily and Tunisia . . .

The harbor of Bizerte after an Allied bombing raid. One large transport lies on her side in shallow water, while other craft, clearly visible from the air above, lie submerged in deeper water.

298. . . . Allied air forces downed 147 transport planes . . .

An Axis air convoy of 35 planes is engaged over the Sicilian Straits by a formation of USAAF B-25 Mitchell bombers, escorted by P-38 Lightnings. In this picture the eye of the camera has caught 12 of the enemy planes flying low and being riddled by machine-gun fire. At extreme left, an American plane has just dived and completed an attack, while another B-25, overhead, awaits its turn to dive. Score in this engagement: 25 enemy planes downed. In similar actions, 96 big Junkers transports loaded with troop reinforcements for North Africa were sent hurtling into the Mediterranean in two eventful days.

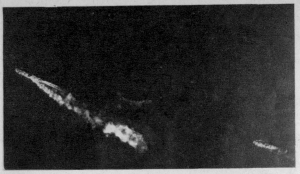

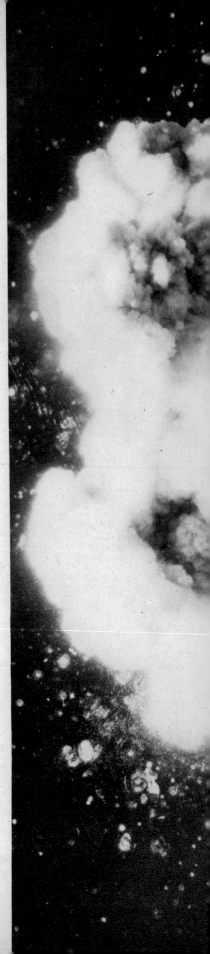

299. . . . damaged or destroyed 31 vessels . . .

This photograph, together with the next three, tell a remarkably graphic story of a single action. Here, two Axis supply ships are sighted by Flying Fortresses in the Mediterranean, off Bizerte.

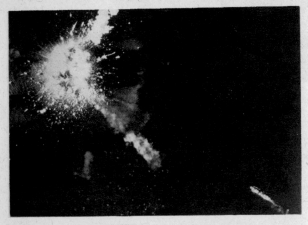

300. . . . and abruptly . . .

Bombs strike the leading vessel, a 6,000-tonner.

301. . . . ruptured Axis communications . . .

The bomb bursts on the first enemy ship are followed by internal explosions, which indicate that it was carrying munitions. Meanwhile, a direct hit is scored on the second vessel.

302. . . . with their Tunisian forces.

Two down is the score as billows of smoke rise and spread from what is left of both ships. Flying Fortresses thus dispose of tons of enemy ammunition which was destined for use against our men.

303. On land the Allied armies took Sfax . . . Kairouan . . . Sousse . . . Mateur.

Hill 609, natural Tunisian fortress, blocks the path of American forces in their final drive for Bizerte.

304. The American 34th Division stormed and captured Hill 609.

Arab village perched on top of Hill 609. Roofless walls show the effect of artillery bombardment. The capture of this strong point cleared the way for our final objective.

305. Then, on May 7, in a 9-mile thrust, the American 2nd Corps seized the big naval base of Bizerte, . . .

Nazi Gen. von Broitch, prisoner of war, crosses the threshold of Allied headquarters after his capture at Bizerte. Preceding him is Gen. Cramer, who commanded all Panzer Divisions in North Africa.

306. . . . entering the city on the same day that the British 8th Army captured Tunis.

Happy townsfolk line the narrow streets to welcome victorious Allied troops as they enter Tunis, their equipment decorated with flowers and leafy branches.

307. This double thrust bottled up the retreating Nazis.

Civilian reaction to the Allied armies is clearly indicated when a joyful father lifts his small daughter onto an armored car and jumps aboard himself, giving the V-for-Victory salute.

308. The Axis armies were now herded into the Cape Bon Peninsula, . . .

These are rescued Russian soldiers who, captured on the Eastern Front, had been sent to North Africa as a labor battalion for the German Army, which used them for digging ditches, trenches, and gun emplacements.

310. On May 13, 1943, the last enemy elements surrendered unconditionally.

Captured German and Italian generals in an Allied transport plane.

309. . . . last Axis corner in Africa.
Attempted evacuation of Axis troops from
the peninsula was largely frustrated by Allied air and sea power, so this Italian soldier
died with his back to the sea. He was a
member of one of the last Axis units to give
battle to the Allies on Cape Bon.

311. Fifteen picked Axis divisions fell into the Allied bag.

Italian Gen. Costa at an Allied Air Force headquarters after his surrender.

312. It was one of the great mass surrenders of fully equipped troops in modern history.

Aerial view of a camp for German prisoners of war, near Mateur. Axis surrendered 252,514 men in addition, lost 30,000 killed 26,400 wounded. This total loss personnel, amounting to more 300,000, compared with Allied ualties of 70,000, of whom 18 were American. The Axis also 1,795 planes and a large qua of other equipment.

313. The Allies buried their dead ...

Pvt. Donald G. McQuarrie, of Thompsonville, Conn., stands solemnly before the grave of a comrade in the American-British El Alia Cemetery, near Algiers.

314. ... and paused a moment for the next act in history's greatest drama.

An Army band gives a concert, with the bomb-wrecked front of a building providing box seats for the audience.

The Axis had now lost an army, a campaign, a continent, and the initiative. The Mediterranean was again open to Allied shipping, which, by shortening the route, meant the equivalent of adding 240 new vessels to our war equipment. American troops had gained experience and demonstrated their efficiency in battle. Allied air forces had mastered a technique of coordination with ground forces and the strategic application of air power. Unity of Allied effort, command, and staff had been effected, tested, and found good. The United Nations were now poised to launch more direct attacks on the southern face of the European Fortress.

THE CAMPAIGN IN SICILY

315. There was no mistaking what the Allies had in mind after North Africa.

A big American bomber flies through bursts of flak to release its bombs on Axis installations in Sicily.

316. With systematic purpose our airmen concentrated on airfields, harbors, and communications . . .

Bombs rain down from a Flying Fortress on Monserrato airfield, near Cagliari in Sardinia.

317. . . . in Sicily, Sardinia, I* and . . .

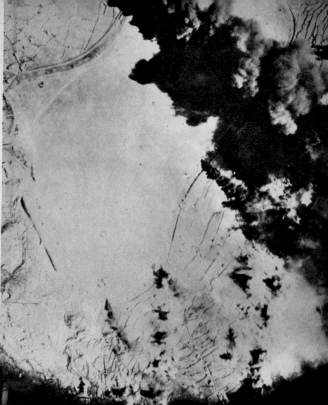

Milo airdrome, in Sicily, is completely covered with bomb bursts, rendering it useless and knocking out more than half of the enemy aircraft caught on the field when the USAAF attack started.

318. . . . Pantelleria — where it was demonstrated that a stronghold can be reduced to surrender by air bombardment.

Precision bombing of Pantelleria airdrome which destroyed installations, runways, and planes on the ground. After concentrated bombing like this, the island surrendered on June 11, 1943 and 10,000 enemy troops were taken prisoner. Adjacent islands also surrendered in quick succession:

Lampedusa on June 12
Linosa on June 13
Lampione on June 14.

319. While our airmen were steadily pulverizing enemy installations . . .

At their base in North Africa, these gunners of a record-breaking Flying Fortress crew give their version of the victory symbol to show that they have accounted for 17 enemy planes. Left to right, all sergeants: William M. Campble, Cuba, Ill.; Leo Robbins, Los Angeles; E. R. Worthy, Eldon, Mo.; Benjamin F. Warmer, San Francisco (with top score of 9); Edward Jackson, Boston; and Carlton McGee, Laurel, Del.

320. . . . the tough veterans of the North African campaign . . .

Lt. Gen. George S. Patton, Jr., designated to command the American invasion troops in Sicily, addresses field officers of the 82nd Airborne Division at Oujda, Morocco, during rehearsal maneuvers.

321. . . . were practising

Streaming down both ramps of their LCI (Landing Craft, Infantry), these infantrymen practise invasion tactics in a landing at Port-aux-Poules, Algeria.

322. ... all the maneuvers of invasion ...

Heavily equipped men clambering up a beach ridge at Arzew, Algeria.

← 323. ... in preparation for D Day.

Paratroops of the 82nd Airborne Division give a mass demonstration of their tactics at Oujda airport.

324. When D Day dawned on July 10, 1943 . . .

In a North African port, assault troops board Higgins boats massed for the invasion of Sicily.

325. . . . more than 3,000 vessels of all sizes, loaded with 160,000 American, British, and Canadian troops . . .

Units of the 3rd Division march onto invasion barges at the port of Bizerte, ready to shove off for Sicily.

326. . . . closed in under formidable air and sea cover . . .

In the early morning of July 10, this invasion barge makes for shore at Gela, Sicily.

327. . . . on 100 miles of Sicily's coastline.

Scores of our boats, mostly transports and landing craft, crowd in toward the southeastern coast of Sicily. This picture, made from a reconnaissance plane, shows shell bursts from land batteries exploding near our ships at lower right.

328. In a hail of enemy fire...
An American convoy off Gela is
bombed by German planes.

**329. ... the American 7th Army un-
der Gen. Patton ...**
In the gray light of early morning, American troops seize beaches near Licata,
Sicily. Smoke on the hilltop is from our
fire.

330. . . . landed with all its equipment . . .

Army mules come ashore with American troops at Licata to do their necessary part in invasion.

331. . . . at various points on the south coast . . .

American soldiers stake down mats on a Sicilian beach to facilitate the landing of heavy vehicles.

332. . . . while the British 8th Army and Canadian forces seized other points on the east coast.

334. . . . and some of them had paid the ultimate price for their courage.

A group of dead American paratroopers found by our advancing infantry just as the enemy had left them.

avy vehicles come ashore at Li-
a despite enemy gunfire. A shell
s just fallen in the shallow water
shore.

333. The night before the ships arrived, our paratroops had landed to take the sting out of enemy resistance . . .

These paratroopers take a well-earned rest after raiding Gela airport and returning safely to one of our beachheads.

335. But the enemy, too . . .
Dead German in Sicily.

336. . . . began to pay a price in men . . .
Another dead German, killed at the wheel of his truck.

338. . . . and matériel . . .
An American soldier tries to rescue the pilot of this German plane, brought down in flames at Gela.

337. . . . as well as in territory . . .
American M-4 and M-5 tanks fire from a Sicilian valley at a pillbox on a hill. It fell soon afterwards.

339. . . . as Allied troops advanced . . .
After taking their beachhead, these American troops move swiftly inland.

340. . . . and smashed their way through the island . . .

North of Raffadali, a mountain road blocked by the retreating Italians is blasted open again by U. S. engineers.

341. ...taking town after town: Licata...Ragusa...Syracuse...

A motorized American unit advances through the streets of Gela, past the wreckage of Italian tanks that had been blown up by our guns.

342. ... Augusta ... Agrigento ... Enna.

Occupation of Sicilian towns with a minimum of damage to landmarks and statues of historic significance sometimes proved of direct assistance to U. S. Army forces. This classic goddess aided the Allies by holding field wire used by American troops at Agrigento.

343. Sometimes our victories came cheaply ...

A wrecked German car and its dead driver beside a road in Sicily.

344. . . . but at other times, as at Gela and Troina, we had to pay a price in blood.

In Santa Agata, U. S. soldiers sweep for mines beside the body of a comrade who was killed by a booby-trap attached to a gate. Three others were killed at this spot, and 20 were injured.

345. On July 22, the Allies took Palermo, Sicily's largest city . . .

In the public square of Palermo, crowds cheer and applaud the "invading" Americans. Said President Roosevelt: "The unmistakably sincere welcome given to the Allied troops by the Italian people has proved conclusively that even in a country which has lived for a generation under a complete dictatorship—with all of its propaganda, censorship, and suppression of free speech and discussion—the love of liberty was unconquerable."

346. . . . thus cutting the island in two and trapping 45,000 Axis soldiers in western Sicily.

On this Sicilian road, a truck loaded with fleeing Italian soldiers hit one of their own mines, and an American jeep, pursuing it, hit another mine. Here the Italian dead and dying lie beside the road while doctors dress the wounds of an American officer standing near the damaged jeep.

347. Civilians in Sicily kne[w] that the coming of the Alli[es] meant food . . .

A boy takes home all the bre[ad] he can carry from an America[n] field kitchen near Trapani.

348. . . . and humanity . . .

After a Nazi air attack, U. S. [En]gineers rescue a family from t[he] ruins of their home at Palma [di] Montechiaro.

349. . . . and freedom.

When the Allied Military Gov[ern]men assumed control over the is[land] of Favignana, off the west coa[st of] Sicily near Trapani, it released p[olit]ical prisoners of the Fascist reg[ime] who had been held there. The [ex]pression on the emaciated fac[e of] this political prisoner registers [in]credulity as he is told that he is [once] more a free man.

350. From Palermo, the American 7th Army now turned and pushed eastward . . .

Cpl. Robert Evelyn, left, of Redlands, Calif., and Pfc. Charles C. Sparlins of Vancouver, Wash., ride a foot-propelled railroad vehicle in Sicily.

351. . . . to effect a junction with the British 8th Army . . .

Tired and foot-weary from his march to Brolo, Sgt. Norwood Dorman of Benson, N. C., falls into the pose of the statue in this memorial to the Italian soldier of World War I.

352. . . . and to drive the Axis from the last corner of Sicily.

A dead German lies where he fell.

353. In two weeks after our first landings, the Allied armies had captured so much of Sicily that Mussolini's government collapsed.

In Santa Agata, half a mile behind the front lines, Pfc. Harvey White of Minneapolis administers blood plasma to a wounded soldier while barefooted civilians look on.

354. With the enemy in full retreat along both coastal roads, Randazzo fell before a united thrust by the British and Americans.

Americans of the 1st Infantry Division take time out to rest on the steps of a church after occupying Nicosia. After the capture of Troina, our forces on the north coast, supported by heavy U. S. naval units, surprised the enemy with a daring amphibious raid in which they took 1,500 prisoners and which landed them behind the Axis lines near Torrenova.

355. On Aug. 17, the Allies came thundering into Messina . . .

The bombing of Messina harbor before our ground troops took the city.

356. . . . three miles across the strait from the mainland of Italy . . .

With an American medium tank in the background as a visible sign of his deliverance, this citizen of Messina welcomes U. S. troops with open arms. The scene is typical of many enacted throughout Sicily as advancing Allied units occupied town after town long under Fascist rule.

357. . . . and all Axis resistance on the island ceased.

From the moment of the first landings, it had taken only 38 days to bring the Sicilian campaign to a successful conclusion. Here, Pvt. Nick Cucinotti of Philadelphia expresses his appreciation of the 155 mm. rifle, known as the "Long Tom," for its effective work against the Axis.

358. Allied losses in killed, wounded, and missing were 31,158 . . .

Wounded men are transferred from jeeps to barges for evacuation to a hospital ship.

359. . . . and of this number the American forces lost 7,445.
American wounded safe aboard a barge at Gela, Sicily.

360. The casualties among the 405,000 Italians . . .

A group of Italians, not a bit downhearted, trudges into a small town near Messina under hastily rigged flags of surrender.

361. ... and Germans ...

A German soldier who has been shot through the head falls into American hands and receives first aid from one of our "medics" in the field.

362. ... were approximately 165,000 ...

A temporary prison camp for captured Axis soldiers at Gela. The Sicilian campaign resulted in the entire destruction of the Italian 6th Army. The Italian 1st, 5th, and 10th Armies had crumbled in Tunisia, and the 8th was blasted to bits by the Russians. Thus five Italian armies were put out of commission. The Germans lost 2 divisions in Sicily.

363. . . . including 132,000 prisoners.

Italian prisoners being loaded onto a boat at Gela for ship-
ment out of Sicily to a permanent prison camp in the U. S. A.
The casualty figures given here do not include many thousands of Italian soldiers who got out of the war by changing
into civilian clothes; nor do the figures include the many
Nazis who were sent to watery graves during their attempted flight across the Straits of Messina.

**364. Now that the enemy had become
extinct in Sicily . . .**

A dead Nazi in Sicily.

365. . . . the stage was set for the next operation . . .

A formation of USAAF B-26 Marauders over Stromboli Island, north of Sicily, after completing a bombing mission in Italy.

366. . . . and the next objective was Italy itself!

Allied chiefs observe the effects of U. S. artillery fire directed across the Straits of Messina against the Italian mainland. Right to left: Gen. Dwight D. Eisenhower, Gen. Sir Bernard L. Montgomery, and Commander Harry Butcher, U. S. Naval Aide to Gen. Eisenhower. Gen. Eisenhower summed up the results of the Sicilian campaign as follows:

1. Sicily had been occupied for use as an Allied base.
2. Our Mediterranean sea route had been protected.
3. The morale of the enemy was damaged because he had at last been beaten on his home grounds.

THE CAMPAIGN IN ITALY

367. Italy did not have long to wait. On Sept. 3, 1943, the British 8th Army stormed across the Strait of Messina to gain a firm toehold on the tip of the Italian peninsula, taking Reggio di Cal·abria and Scilla the first day.

While Sicilian children watch from a beach near Messina, a convoy of American-made "ducks," owned and used by the British, leaves with supplies and equipment for the 8th Army. Farther out, Allied landing barges and warships are silhouetted against the Italian mainland.

368. On the same day, in Sicily, the Italian Government signed a secret military armistice with the Allies, effective 5 days later.

Lt. Gen. Aldo Castillani, the representative of the Italian Government, shakes hands with Gen. Eisenhower after signing the armistice. At extreme left, Maj. Gen. Walter B. Smith, Chief of Staff to Gen. Eisenhower, holds the document in his hands. The signing took place at advanced Allied headquarters in Sicily.

369. While the British 8th Army extended its hold on southern Italy, the Americans prepared for landings of their own ...

A stick of heavy bombs hurtles down on Capodichino airfield, Naples, in a raid by Flying Fortresses of the Northwest African Air Force.

370. ... by bombing the Naples area with intense concentration ...

After dropping its bombs on Naples, this Flying Fortress has just been hit by flak which blew off one wing and turned the ship completely over. In spite of this, the sturdy ship managed to level off 1,500 feet lower, a few minutes after this picture was taken, and 5 parachutes were seen to open.

371. . . . and by assembling a huge armada . . .

At Palermo, Sicily, this group of LSTs waits at
the dock to take on American troops and their
equipment. Jeeps, tanks, trucks, and men are
easily loaded and unloaded through the huge
bow openings. Overhead, barrage balloons
hover for protection against enemy air attacks.

**372. . . . to transport the American 5th
Army under Lt. Gen. Mark W. Clark.**

At other docks in Palermo, these U. S. troops
line up to board still more ships that will take
them to the Italian mainland.

373. On Sept. 8, the news of the Italian armistice was flashed to the world in three words: "ITALY SURRENDERS UN-CONDITIONALLY!"

Aboard their transports, U. S. troops cheer the news.

374. The same day, the American 5th Army landed at various points south of Naples...

A combat team of the 43rd Infantry Regiment dashes ashore under protection of strong units of the American and British fleets. The naval vessels softened up the landing points by shelling enemy shore positions.

375. ...and established their beachheads, some of them in the face of stiff German opposition.

Having secured their position on the beach, these U. S. Infantrymen move cautiously forward to engage the enemy for the first time on the soil of the Italian mainland.

376. The heaviest enemy resistance was encountered around Salerno...

In a pause between outbursts of German artillery fire, our troops advance behind a wall.

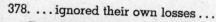

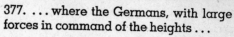

377. . . . where the Germans, with large forces in command of the heights . . .

A combat team of U. S. Engineers moves cautiously through ruined streets.

378. . . . ignored their own losses . . .

The advance of the 3rd Infantry Division saw many scenes such as this one—dead German soldiers, placed on litters by the roadside, in preparation for burial.

379. . . . in order to inflict large casualties on the Americans.

Sgt. R. Strebe, from the State of Washington, checks the bodies of American soldiers killed in action.

380, 381, 382. The American 5th Army fought back savagely.

(380) A camouflaged 8-inch howitzer of a Field Artillery Battalion is fired at night during an offensive against a German strong point.

(381) The gun crew of a similar howitzer is silhouetted against the flash as it fires.

(382) A battery of American big guns helps lay down one of the heaviest artillery concentrations of the war to support the advance of the 36th Infantry Division.

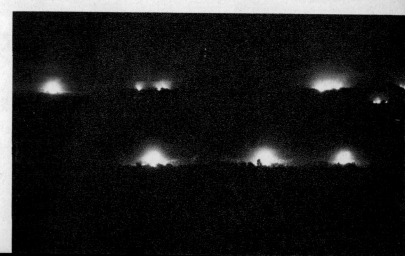

383. By Sept. 16, Lt. Gen. Clark was able to say, in an order of the day: "Our beachhead is secure . . .

As American infantrymen advance through a vegetable patch, one of their number stoops to examine the crop.

384. ". . . Additional troops are landing every day . . .

A convoy unloading men and supplies near Agropoli.

385. "... and we are here to stay."

These German prisoners realize that, for them at least, the jig is up, as Pvt. Lyle Lane, of Chatfield, Minn., inspects their equipment.

386. The next day, the British 8th Army, which had already captured Taranto, Brindisi, and Bari ...

Gen. Eisenhower, while touring the Italian front, stops in Grazziane to talk to British soldiers in a Bren carrier.

387. ...effected a junction with the American 5th Army.

American and British reconnaissance units make contact in the Italian hills near Mercato.

388. Meanwhile, the Germans had occupied Rome and all of northern Italy.

The Northwest African Air Force undertakes precision bombing of the San Lorenzo railroad yards in Rome, taking extreme precautions to destroy only military installations. The Germans were pouring reinforcements through Rome from the north to meet the Allied invasion in the south.

389. During the rest of September, heavy fighting developed ...

A battery crew rams a 155-mm. shell into the breech of their "Long Tom" to fire at German emplacements dug into the mountainside opposite.

390. ... in the mountain barrier between Salerno and Naples.

American white-phosphorus shells burst on a German-held hill. U. S. infantrymen advanced against the enemy positions under the partial cover of this smoke screen.

391. As the Germans were pushed back...

Members of the 3rd Infantry Division advance along a mountain road, past the body of a dead German soldier.

392. ...they systematically destro[y] roads and bridges as they went.

The Nazis blasted this bridge near O[l]
Citra, so our supply column has to for[ce a]
stream.

393. These demolitions . . .

U. S. Engineers replace a bridge blown up by the Nazis on the road between Battipaglia and Acerno.

394. . . . aided by the rugged terrain . . .

A rifle squad of Rangers covers the advance of an assault unit, out of sight on the hillside below.

395. . . . and stubborn ene-my rear-guard actions . . .

An infantry patrol, searching for concealed snipers of the German rear guard, advances warily into the outskirts of a town in the mountains.

396. . . . slowed the American advance.

Over rubble and wreckage, past ruined buildings, American troops move into Avellino.

397. The end of September was the end of the Nazis in Naples.

Railway yards, sheds, and rolling stock severely damaged by Allied bombing raids on Naples before Americans entered the city. As the Nazis withdrew, they looted everything they could carry away and demolished the port's facilities, scuttling 30 ships in the harbor. U. S. Engineers had to repair the railroads, remove the wreckage from the harbor, and restore the docks. Soon deep-draft vessels were able to tie up and unload quickly, thus solving the supply problem of the 5th Army.

398. Shortly after dawn on Oct. 1, 5th Army troops entered the city.

Arriving at their rest camp in Naples, these American soldiers gather around an officer to receive instructions on how to conduct themselves in the city. Many of the men are still wearing field packs and carrying rifles. Some also have blanket rolls, indicating that they have not yet set up their camp.

399. The Germans re-treated northward, leaving devastation in their wake...

A U. S. half-track passes a burning house which has just been hit by an enemy dive bomber.

400. ... and took up strong positions in what they hoped would be their winter line, along the Volturno River.

Mitchell medium bombers wheel over a German encampment along the Volturno. Bombs from other planes in the formation are bursting on Nazi gun emplacements.

1, 402. As enemy resistance stiffened, Allied air power struck at y points in German-occupied Italy, such as Leghorn . . .

(401) An important oil refinery, center, at Leghorn, is the target of these 500-pound bombs.

(402) The oil tanks explode as the bombs find their mark. Of 12 enemy aircraft which attempted to intercept this mission, one was shot down and two were damaged. All of our planes returned to their bases.

403. ... Rome ...

In this surprise attack on the Ciampino airfield near Rome,
many German planes are caught on the ground and destroyed.
As this picture shows, the bomb bursts have blanketed the field.

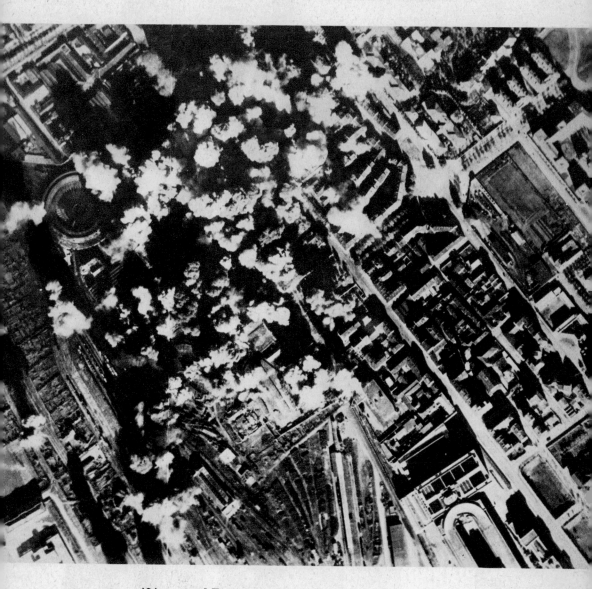

404. . . . and Turin

A ball-bearing manufacturing plant and adjacent railroad yards are seriously damaged by this raid on Turin. Loss of facilities for making ball bearings greatly hampers the enemy's mechanized forces, both on the ground and in the air.

405. On the ground, the Allies were pushing ahead ...

Big guns, drawn by tractors, cross a pontoon bridge on their way to the front.

406. ... in the face of many obstacles.

Trucks loaded with ammunition churn through a lake of soupy mud to supply the guns at the front.

407. On Oct. 13, Italy declared war on Germany...

Italian Maj. Luigi Ottino, right, talks to German prisoners in a stockade at Taranto. Maj. Ottino led the capture of 11 German officers and 422 soldiers by Italian troops on the island of Corfu, whence the prisoners were transported by fishing boats across the Adriatic. Other Italian troops chased the German garrison out of Sardinia.

408. ... and was accepted as a co-belligerent by the United States, Great Britain, and the Soviet Union.

An Italian soldier, Pvt. Andreeto Luciano, left, helps an American soldier, Pvt. Gabriel Musella, of Brooklyn, to lay field wire in a sector where units of both armies are working together.

409. Next day, the Allies established a bridgehead across the Volturno River...

A light tank, attempting to ford the Volturno, is pulled to safety by a bulldozer.

410. ... and were now 100 miles from Rome.

Crew of a half-track keeps on the alert for an enemy air attack.

411. As America's second year of war drew to a close, Allied troops were fighting rain, ...

Pfc. George Denmeade, Jr., of Struthers, O., anti-aircraft gunner with the 5th Army, bails "Italian sunshine" out of his gun pit, a regular morning chore.

412. . . . mud, . . .

A large U. S. truck bogs down in the Capua sector.

413. . . . still more mud, . . .

Cpl. Isom Milorn, of Pineville, Ore., uses his bulldozer to shove the mire aside on "the road to Rome."

414. . . . cold, . . .

Paratroops eat their Thanksgiving dinner in a cold rain.

415. ... mountain terrain, ...

These 155-mm. howitzers have just been towed up a bank through sticky mud in the Colli sector, and now they go into action against the enemy beyond the hills.

416. ... and a reinforced enemy ...

An American truck burning beside a road in the Cassino sector after being hit by shells from a Focke-Wulf 190 during a strafing raid.

417. . . . but nothing could weaken their determination to take Fortress Europe.

Gen. Eisenhower and Gen. Clark study a map at an advanced Allied post. Reviewing the campaign since the North African landings, Secretary Stimson said, on Armistice Day, 1943: "Constantly maintaining their speed and momentum, our forces have now reached the continental mainland of Italy, have shorn the Axis of one of its principal partners, have gained possession of most of the Italian fleet, and have reduced the once invincible German army to the defensive. Our troops have captured over 468,000 prisoners during these campaigns and our air forces have destroyed more than 4,000 enemy aircraft at a cost of only 1,800 of our own. These events will rank with any military accomplishments in our annals. To these men of Gen. Eisenhower's armies, I express my profound admiration for their undying deeds."

IV

THE CAMPAIGN IN THE AIR
OVER EUROPE

THE story of the air war over Europe really begins early in the
fall of 1940, when the skies over Britain were filled with the
noise of hostile planes and the nights were red with the flames
of burning cities. The Luftwaffe was trying to win control of the
air over Britain in order to destroy Britain's will to continue fighting. Both efforts failed; the dogged courage of Britain's people
and the superb skill of the RAF never faltered.

With the new year came a turn in the air war over Europe. In
1941 the offensive passed from German hands, and the RAF began to carry the war to Germany, with the bombing of her industries on a scale which was to surpass all German efforts to blitz
England. The Reich declared war on the United States in Decem-
ber, 1941, but it took time and hard work to prepare for the day
when American air power would begin to play its part over
Europe. The difficult problem of supplying materiel, equipment,
and personnel to the installations made available for the American forces in the British Isles was solved by a tremendous pro-
gram of shipping and construction.

On July 4, 1942, American bombers made their first raid on
western Europe. During the next six months the tempo of their
blows increased, as they gained experience and felt out the
enemy, mostly with daylight precision attacks—the accurate,
deadly type of bombing which was to become America's greatest and most valuable contribution to air war.

In 1943 the United Nations' air attack on Germany shifted into
high. While British bombers pounded whole cities in night raids,
American planes went after important targets in daylight at-

tacks. In January, Wilhelmshaven and Emden gained distinction by being the first German towns to be bombed by the USAAF. In March our airmen made attacks on Lorient and Brest, Rouen and Essen, Vegesack and Rotterdam; in April, Mannheim and Pilsen joined the list; in May, Kiel and Antwerp. On August 1, Ploesti and Campina, where Rumania's largest oil refineries are situated, were subjected to what has been termed "the biggest low-level mass raid in history," by 165 B-24's of the 9th Air Force. Less than 2 weeks later 100 Liberators flew from bases in northwest Africa to bomb the Messerschmitt factory at Wiener Neustadt.

As the Allied drive gathered momentum, German opposition stiffened; more and more fighter plane strength, sorely needed on other fronts, was withdrawn to protect the west of Germany.

One of the greatest air battles in history took place on October 14, when nearly 350 Flying Fortresses of the 8th USAAF attacked the ball-bearing factory in Schweinfurt, encountering between 300 and 400 enemy fighters. The cost in men and planes was high, but as a result of this one attack it is estimated that about 50 per cent of Germany's total production of ball bearings was cut off. Moreover, the enemy's losses amounted to 125 planes.

As 1943 ended, the stage was set for the last act. Much had already been accomplished, both in material damage and in the undermining of German morale. Now our ground troops awaited the day when their part in the invasion of Europe would begin.

In the words of General Arnold: "The Fortresses that daily cross the Channel are building a bridge for the invasion of Europe. They have opened a battlefront 20,000 feet over the heads of the German people."

Scale of Miles
0   100   200

ATLANTIC

OCEAN

Coruña

B.
B.

PORTUGAL
Lisbon
Sevilla
SPAI
Mad
INTERNAT'L ZONE
Gibraltar
Ceuta
MOROCCO
Oran

MOROCCO

A

THE C
IN THE
EUI

418. When Gen. Marshall submitted to the nation his first report on global war, he listed 43 overseas stations to which American troops had been sent.

A conference in the War Department. Seated, left to right: Lt. Gen. (now Gen.) Henry H. Arnold, Gen. George C. Marshall, Lt. Gen. Lesley J. McNair; standing, left to right: Maj. Gen. (now Lt. Gen.) Joseph T. McNarney, and Maj. Gen. (now Lt. Gen.) Brehon B. Somervell.

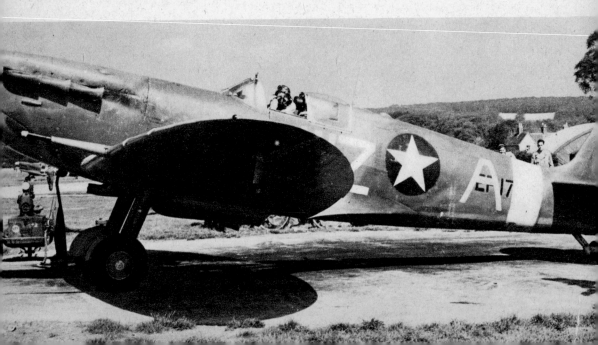

419. Among the most important of these overseas stations was the British Isles, where the first American planes...

A P-38 Lockheed Lightning is carefully hoisted from the hold of a transport "somewhere in England." Many planes, of course, were flown across.

420. ...and American crews to fly them, arrived on Jan. 26, 1942.

A Spitfire squadron on the alert. This picture shows the first U. S. squadron to use Spitfires in England.

421, 422, 423. Our airmen had to be trained intensively for a new type of aerial warfare, which Gen. Marshall explained thus: "The British heavy bomber command was developed for the purpose of carrying out night missions, while the American Flying Fortresses and Liberators were developed for daylight operations. . . .

(421) American bomber crews in England gather for a briefing session before a flight.

(422) Bombing up a Flying Fortress at a USAAF base in England.

(423) Ground crews wave good luck to a Fortress as it takes of

424, 425, 426. ". . . In the British planes, speed and armament were limited in favor of long range and heavy bomb loads. This type plane is especially effective for night operations over industrial areas where a high degree of precision in bombing is not vitally necessary. . . .

(424) This gun is mounted on a swivel, and the gunner learns on the ground how to maneuver it. He must keep his elbows in and his head close to the butt, so that he can always hold the sights in line.

(425) This is the first bomb that was ever loaded under an American fighter plane in England. Left to right: Sgt. Carl E. Trabin, Philadelphia; Cpl. Loren Toycer, Colfax, Wis.; Sgt. William Woods, Baltimore; and Lt. Herbert K. Fields.

(426) Loading a fighter.

427, 428, 429. "...On the other hand, the American bomber design tends toward a fast, very heavily armed and armored high-altitude plane. Its more limited bomb capacity is compensated for by the perfection of the precision bombsight which permits small specific targets to be singled out for destruction."

(427) A U. S. bomber crew at their base in England. First row, left to right: Lt. R. W. Smith, Pomona, Calif.; Lt. C. G. Jones, Lima, O.; Cpl. R. R. Banks, Easton, Mass.; Sgt. H. E. Warren, Benton Harbor, Mich. Second row, left to right: Lt. F. D. Gillogly, Alperville, Ill.; Sgt. L. V. Edwards, Phoenix, Ariz.; Sgt. W. Allen, San Francisco; Sgt. C. F. Fehr, Madille, Okla.; and Sgt. J. W. Haywod, Dublin, Ga.

430. The USAAF assault on the continent of Europe began July 4, 1942, when American planes and crews participated in an RAF attack.

Sgt. Harris Goldberg, of Brookline, Mass., had completed 42 missions with the RAF before he was transferred to the USAAF and flew as tail gunner in this Flying Fortress, which was hit by 20-mm. cannon fire over enemy territory. Back at its base, 12 other Fortresses fly in formation overhead.

(428) Upon returning from an operation, the crew questioned by an intelligence officer.

(429) American airmen in England use bicycles to go back and forth between their ships, their school, and their quarters.

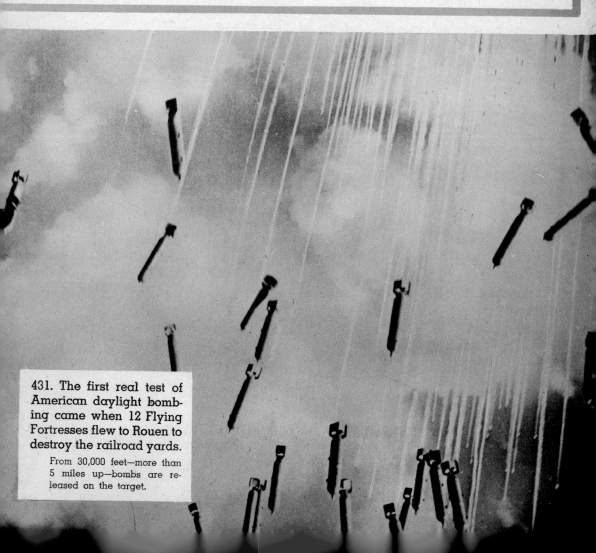

431. The first real test of American daylight bombing came when 12 Flying Fortresses flew to Rouen to destroy the railroad yards.

From 30,000 feet—more than 5 miles up—bombs are released on the target.

432. The Rouen mission was successful, and all ships returned to their base.

The earth feels good to the crew of "Hell's Angels" as they bring her back safely.

433. Oct. 9, 1942 saw the first large-scale bombing by the 8th Air Force, based in Britain, when heavy bombers set out for Lille.

Part of a formation of Fortresses en route to their target.

434. On this raid, our airmen downed 25 Nazi planes, probably downed 38 others, and damaged 44.

Lille, city of heavy industries. Sticks of bombs are bursting across the Fives-Lille Steel and Engineering Works. Adjoining locomotive and freight-car repair shops are also heavily damaged.

435. And it was over Lille that American bombers first met heavy Nazi resistance.

A Fortress falls out of formation and hurtles earthward, with smoke issuing from its motors and its vertical fin and horizontal stabilizer shot off.

436. American air operations over Europe in 1942 accomplished much: . . .

One of a group of Martin B-26 Marauder medium bombers makes its run over a Nazi airdrome at Tricqueville, France. This was the home base of the famed Goering "Yellow Nosed" Fighter Squadron. In this raid, hangars, repair shops, and dispersal areas were blasted by dozens of sticks of 300-pound bombs.

437. (a) Although Germany had abandoned daylight bombing after losing 185 planes in one day over Britain, the USAAF went ahead in the face of skepticism and proved the value of precision bombing by daylight.

The Renault plant in Paris had been manufacturing trucks for the Nazis. This is the foundry of the plant after American high-altitude precision bombers dropped their calling cards.

438. (b) American airmen felt out the enemy and gained experience in combat.

Capt. Walker Mahurin, age 24, of Fort Wayne, Ind., top-scoring fighter of the 8th Air Force, receives congratulations from a fellow pilot on returning from a combat mission in which he shot down 3 enemy planes. His squadron's goal of 100 Nazi planes to be bagged by a certain date was reached 50 days before the date set.

439. (c) The stage was set for what was soon to come—the greatest aerial offensive the world had ever seen.

At the start of an important mission, formations of American "heavies" fill the cold upper air, trailing comet-like tails caused by vapor condensation.

440. "This," said Gen. Arnold, "is an aerial war in which one or the other of the combatants will be driven from the sky . . .

This American Fortress had its rudder badly damaged during a raid over France on Oct. 9, 1942, but it was brought home with only a few minor injuries to the crew.

441. "...and it won't be us."

The Luftwaffe comes off second best to the U. S. Army 8th Air Force. With bits of wreckage hurtling through the air above it, this twin-engined Nazi plane, fire pouring from its starboard motor, is going down for the count after being hit by Lt. Richard A. Stearns of Augusta, Ga.

442. The all-out offensive began in January 1943...

Bombs are brought up by the armament crews, ready to load at a base in England.

443. ...when the USAAF joined the RAF...

King George talks with American officers at an 8th Air Force base.

444. . . . in a big daylight raid over Germany.

Forty-two of the Flying Fortresses which participated in an attack on Wilhelmshaven.

445. Destination: Wilhelmshaven.

A few moments after this picture was taken, these P-47 Thunderbolts peeled off in flights of 4 to give escort to Flying Fortresses and Liberator bombers on their way to Wilhelmshaven.

446. Target: the U-boat ways.

American bombs descend on the newly opened Adolf Hitler Haven at the great Nazi naval base at Wilhelmshaven.

447. "Our heavy bomber offensive," said Gen. Arnold, "not only destroys vital objectives, . . .

Hanover, Germany. Dense clouds of smoke obscure the target area after rubber factories and adjacent railway installations have been bombed. Two of the plants damaged here produced 80 per cent of Germany's total output of aero tires and other essential rubber products. Strong fighter opposition was encountered on this raid by unescorted Fortresses, which reported shooting down 22 Nazi fighters, with 8 others probably downed, and 22 more damaged.

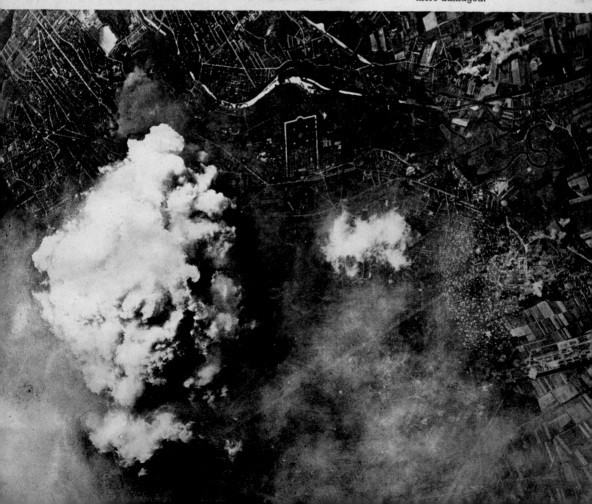

448. "...it also reduces the striking power of the Luftwaffe, and reduces Nazi ability to intercept our ever-increasing bombardments...

Penetration into German-occupied Europe by long-range fighter planes of the U. S. Army 8th Air Force is plotted on this map table, with Air Forces WACS of the European Theatre engaged in charting the course to and from the target area. Left to right: Pfc. Vera Schulte, St. Louis; Pfc. Ann Lege, Fitchburg, Mass.; Corp. Jennie D. Johnson, Miami; and Pfc. Elizabeth Freda, Rankin, Mass.

449. "...These missions are directed toward the total destruction of targets in the heart of Europe where it will hurt the Axis war machine most."

Antwerp, Belgium. A daylight raid on Ford and General Motors plants, converted by the Nazis into major motor shops for the German war machine, inflicts heavy damage. Tons of bombs are dumped on the plants themselves, as well as on adjacent docks, warehouses, and railroad sidings.

450. Said Gen. Marshall: "The violence of the German fighter plane reaction to our daylight attacks is convincing evidence of the deadly effect of precision bombing . . .

Lt. H. E. Miller, of Ridgeland, S. C., saw a German Focke-Wulf 190 fighter nearly blow the tail off the Flying Fortress that was ahead of him in formation. He thought the hole was big enough for him to walk through. (He is 6 feet, 4 inches tall.) Back at the home station, he has a chance to prove that his estimate was correct, for the crippled Fortress returned to its base, and the pilot who brought it in was Lt. Donald E. Stockton, of Redmond, Ore.

451. ". . . The enemy must find a counter to this technique or accept the emasculation of his industries and his fighter command."

Hanover. This reconnaissance photograph of the bombed area (broken white lines) shows that several buildings of Germany's largest rubber factory have been destroyed, the upper stories of the tire molding and assembling plant knocked out, and other parts of the works severely damaged. In addition, the railway tracks and a huge freight station suffered direct hits.

452. To confuse the enemy and disperse his fighter strength, Americans made their first multiple attack on May 14, 1943, hitting 4 targets the same day with 200 bombers.

On this mission, bombs and bombers, flak-bursts and vapor trails, fill the air. From the May 14th raids, 11 of our ships did not come back, but the Nazis lost 67 planes.

453. The American plan of target priorities was simple and definite: ...

On returning from a successful bombing mission, the whole crew of the Fortress appropriately named "Jerry Jinx" gets a ride back to their field headquarters.

454. (a) To relieve the strain on Allied shipping by bombing submarine bases like Wilhelmshaven and St. Nazaire.

St. Nazaire. The submarine pens take a heavy pounding.

455. (b) To knock out Axis aircraft and munitions factories, such as the Focke-Wulf plant at Warnemunde . . .

Warnemunde, Germany. The Arado Flugzeugwerke (formerly the Ernst Heinkel Flugzeugwerke) was concentrating on the production of the Nazi's ace fighter plane, the Focke-Wulf 190, when this attack by Flying Fortresses destroyed or damaged 18 of its 27 buildings. Enemy fighter opposition was described as "very weak."

456, 457. ... and the Messerschmitt plant at Wiener Neustadt.

(456) Wiener Neustadt, Austria, near Vienna. A B-24 Liberator of the 15th Army Air Force wings away from the target after dropping its load and adding its bit to the serious damage inflicted on this important cog in the Nazi war machine.

(457) The same Liberator seen in the preceding picture was hit by heavy flak as it tried to get away, and shows a gaping hole estimated to be 5 by 13 feet. The plane fell shortly after this photograph was taken.

458. (c) To disrupt enemy communications by attacking ports like Dieppe . . .

Fortress "Dixie Demo" brings its crew safely home after a raid on Dieppe.

459. . . . and air bases like Tatoi field in Greece.

Tatoi airfield, near Athens. Bombs dropped by Flying Fortresses of the Northwest African Air Force blossom on the hangars and landing strip, as well as on grounded Nazi planes dispersed around the edge of the field.

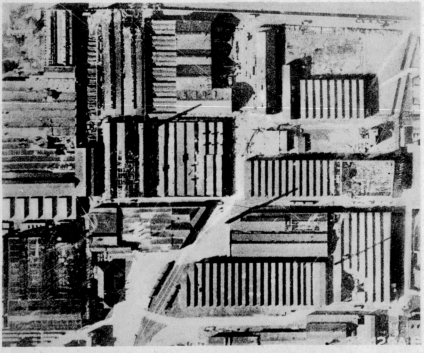

460. Following this plan, the USAAF concentrated on 90 vital Nazi industrial centers.

Hamm, Germany. This reconnaissance photograph shows damage done to the great steel works.

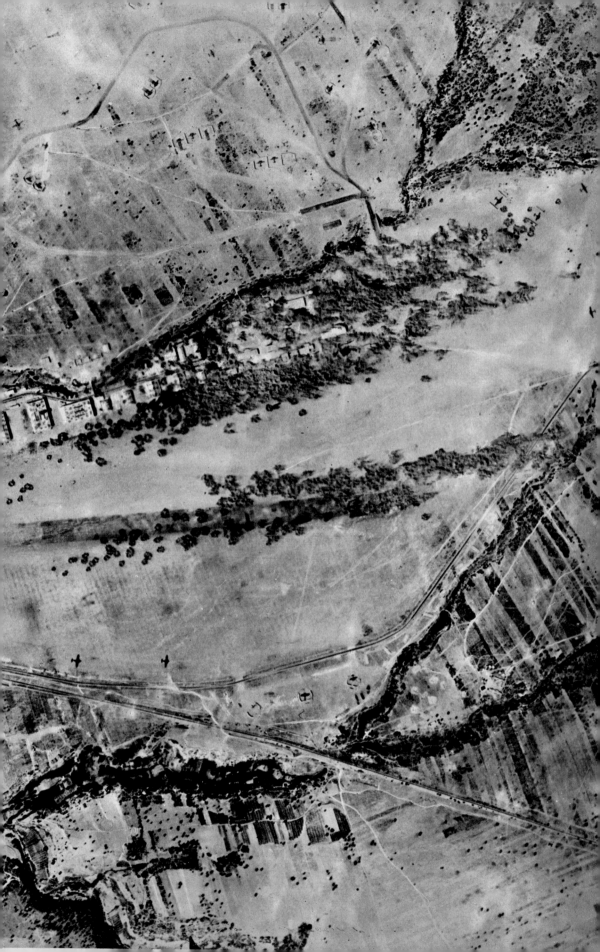

461, 462, 463. On Aug. 1, 1943, American bombers from Africa made an audacious and devastating attack . . .

Coming in at low level, 165 of the 177 B-24 Liberators that started on the mission unload their bombs and knock out an estimated 40 per cent of the production facilities of Rumania's largest oil refineries. In this operation we lost 39 bombers destroyed and 54 others missing or known to be interned. The Nazis lost 51 fighters out of a total of 87 encountered.

464, 465, 466. . . . on the great Nazi oil installations at Ploesti, Rumania.

(464, 465) Heavy as were our losses on this raid, "It cost the Nazis," said President Roosevelt, "half of Rumania's oil production for a full year. I am certain that the German or the Japanese high commands would cheerfully sacrifice tens of thousands of men to do the same amount of damage to us, if they could. Those gallant and brilliant young Americans who raided Ploesti won a smashing victory which, I believe, will contribute materially to the shortening of the war and thus save countless lives."

(466) Col. Leon W. Johnson, of Moline, Kan., shows Lt. Gen. Devers and Lt. Gen. Eaker the score board on one of the Liberators that participated in the attack on Ploesti. The swastikas mean 13 enemy planes downed. The bombs indicate that the plane has been on 28 missions. The horizontal bomb represents the Ploesti attack, so painted to show that they flew so low they "laid" the bombs instead of dropping them.

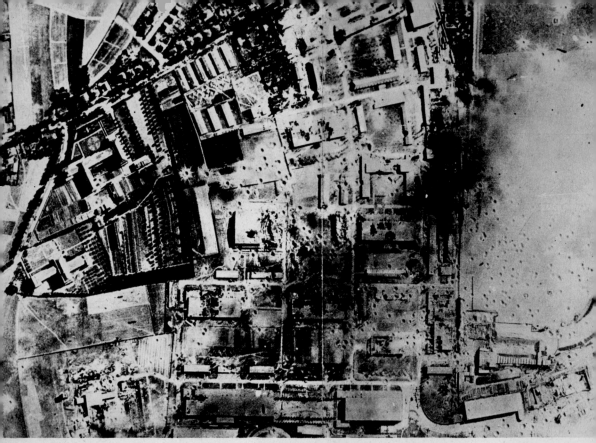

467. Sixteen days later, a powerful task force took off from bases in England and struck deep into Germany to bomb the Messerschmitt factory at Regensburg.

This reconnaissance photograph gives grim evidence of the success of the raid. Leaders of the flight were confident that the target had been destroyed. As the picture shows, nearly all bomb craters are either within the factory boundaries or on the adjacent airfield. Heavy damage has occurred all over the works, almost every building being affected in some degree. As Gen. Arnold said: "The 8th Air Force delivered the bombs to Regensburg and destroyed factories producing more than 200 planes a month."

468. After completing the Regensburg mission, the attacking Fortresses flew on across the Alps and landed in Africa.

On this shuttle raid, the Fortresses fly over 12,000-foot peaks to reach friendly bases in North Africa. "A few days later," said Gen. Arnold, "they returned by way of Bordeaux and successfully bombed a great concentration of enemy planes. The men who flew on that historic mission had to fight their way through clouds of Nazi fighters that rose up in relays across much of their 2,800-mile round trip. Our heavy bombers and fighters shot down 307 Nazi planes in the greatest single day's battle fought by any air force anywhere."

TARGET AREA

469. Hamburg was struck 8 times in 6 days.

Germany's greatest port and second largest city gets it from the RAF by night and from the 8th USAAF by day. Here an area of factories, warehouses, dockyards, and shipping smoulders in the ruin of a thousand fires, sending up a pall of smoke 5 miles high. During these 6 days, 8,000 tons of high explosives rained on Hamburg—more than the total the Luftwaffe dropped on England in the entire 11 months of "blitz" from September 1940 to July 1941. In this picture, silhouetted against the smoke pall, a Focke-Wulf 190 trails far behind several U. S. Fortresses.

470. The largest number of planes . . .

Flying Fortresses. Destination: Bremen.

471. . . . ever to participate in an 8th Air Force mission (up to then) . . .

Through the clouds to Bremen.

472. . . . raided Bremen on Nov. 26, 1943.

Over the city, flak bursts among the attacking Fortresses, and one of them, already hit, falls from the sky (lower right), its severed tail following closely behind. This attack on Bremen scored heavy damage on submarine docks and shipyards.

473. American planes roamed over the Brenner Pass . . .

A 3-plane formation of Fortresses flies over the spot where Hitler and Mussolini had conferred—the gateway between Germany and Italy. Below, the Sill River winds between the peaks that flank the pass.

474. ...and over the French Riviera.

Fortresses of the 12th USAAF drop their bombs on an important viaduct of the coastal railway, 5 miles from Cannes.

475. But of course the primary target of all was...

The road into the heart of Germany is paved with flak—"almost heavy enough," said Gen. Arnold, "to walk on across to Berlin."

476. . . . Berlin!

The Nazi capital is smashed by the RAF into a hell of fire and high explosives. Later they were to be joined by the USAAF.

477, 478, 479, 480. In these important operations, America was paying a price in men and planes.

(477) This series of pictures shows the last moments of a Flying Fortress shot down while nearing the coast of Norway, one of a formation that attacked the Rjukan power station and electro-chemical works. Here the stricken plane twists downward out of control, a parachute blossoming above it.

(478) The falling plane leaves the parachute out of sight above it.

(479) Trailing smoke behind it, the plane levels off momentarily, then plunges downward again.

(480) It crashes into the North Sea.

481. But for the results obtained, it was an incredibly low price.

Estimated results: 2,000 of the enemy's vital industrial plants and 17 important German cities almost entirely in ruins; 6,000,000 Germans made homeless.

482. The world awaited the final assault on Hitler's Fortress Europe "from the east, west, and south"—and from the top.

By November 1943, Allied bombers based in Britain were dropping on enemy territory 200 long tons of explosives for every ton the Luftwaffe dropped on Britain.

Maj. Gen. William E. Kepner, chief of the 8th Air Force Fighter Command, declared that the Luftwaffe had been beaten at every turn, and that the Nazis were no longer capable of building enough fighters to stop the Allied bombing offensive.

In November 1943, America produced more than 1,000 4-engined bombers; it was turning out 338 aircraft daily. In 1944, the expected production figures were 1,500 heavy bombers and 10,000 aircraft of all types monthly.

As America approached the second anniversary of Pearl Harbor, the 8th Air Force, giving its entire attention to Nazi Europe, announced the following box score:

Enemy planes destroyed	3,500*
Own planes destroyed	865*
Enemy planes probably destroyed	1,100
Enemy planes damaged	1,700
Total tons of bombs dropped	42,100
Total combat sorties	52,700

*A favorable ratio of better than 4 to 1.

The USAAF in all theatres had achieved the following totals since Pearl Harbor:

Enemy planes destroyed	9,300
Own planes destroyed	2,512
Enemy planes probably destroyed	2,700
Enemy planes damaged	3,100
Total tons of bombs dropped	164,400
Total combat sorties	341,400

The USAAF found itself ready for what lay ahead with a force of nearly 2,000,000 expertly trained pilots, bombardiers, radio operators, navigators, and technicians. Not far ahead lay its goal of 2,500,000 men and 100,000 planes.